A Pagan Prophet
William Morris

A Pagan Prophet
William Morris

Charlotte H. Oberg

University Press of Virginia

Charlottesville

THE UNIVERSITY PRESS OF VIRGINIA
Copyright © 1978 by the Rector and Visitors
of the University of Virginia

First Published 1978

Library of Congress Cataloging in Publication Data

Oberg, Charlotte H   1936–
  A pagan prophet, William Morris.

  Includes index.
  1.   Morris, William, 1834–1896—Criticism and
interpretation.   I.   Title.
PR5084.02   821'.8   77–4730   ISBN 0–8139–0714–4

Printed in the United States of America

Frontispiece: Sir Edward Burne-Jones: Perseus
Cycle No. 9, *The Doom Fulfilled* (Perseus slays the
serpent). (Courtesy of the Southampton Art
Gallery.)

To Andrew

Contents

Acknowledgments

To Cecil Y. Lang for his continuing inspiration and guidance, I am especially grateful. I have benefited from the advice of many other colleagues and friends, especially Robert L. Kellogg and Joseph R. Dunlap. I am also grateful to Carole Silver, Joseph S. White and Josephine S. McMurtry.

A National Endowment for the Humanities Younger Humanist Fellowship during 1973-74 enabled me to complete much of the specific research for this book in England while enlarging my general understanding of Morris's work. I am also indebted to the University of Richmond for several research grants awarded me during the early stages of this project. Publication of this book has been made possible through the support of the University of Richmond's Faculty Publication Fund. I wish to thank Dean C. J. Gray for his part in making arrangements for this publication.

I owe much to the facilities and services of many different libraries and museums, especially the British Museum Reading Room, The Victoria and Albert Museum, and the Tate Gallery. Not least is my debt to the staff of the University of Richmond's Boatwright Memorial Library.

An early draft of chapter 7 entitled "The Theme of Renewal in Morris's Later Prose Romances" was read to the William Morris Society at the Central School of Art and Design, London, on 9 May 1974, and an abridged version of this same chapter was presented at the Modern Language Association Annual Convention in San Francisco on 28 December 1975 under the title, "Motif and Theme in the Late Prose Romances of William Morris." This paper, along with four other papers on Morris presented at the same convention, has been published in *Studies in the Late Romances of William Morris* (New York: The William Morris Society, 1976).

Introduction

An Enigmatic Victorian

WILLIAM MORRIS—writer, translator, printer, painter, designer, decorator, lecturer, political activist—is one of the most fascinatingly paradoxical figures to emerge in an age of paradox. In the contradictions of his own life he epitomizes the contradictions of a society that saw the world undergo more changes in a shorter time than in any previous epoch. The scion of a prosperous middle-class family, he enjoyed the privilege of wealth in a society learning to accommodate the dominance of his own bourgeois class. Yet he not only spent much of his inherited wealth but devoted the greater part of his mature years to renouncing (and denouncing) the very principles that had enabled him to become a person sufficiently important for his repudiation to be worthwhile. (The wealth itself he did not renounce, for, as he must have realized, his financial independence was what gave him the freedom to put his ideals into practice.) He passionately advocated the obliteration of class distinctions and the equitable distribution of wealth, and he sought to restore art to what he conceived as its rightful historical place—as an integral function of the daily lives of all people. Though a number of items made by Morris & Co., including wallpapers and chintzes as well as rush-bottom chairs, could be bought by people with middle-range incomes, many of the furnishings made by the firm were always too expensive for any but the rich to buy, and in 1880, after his politics had become democratic in the extreme, if not yet quite socialistic, his firm so far cooperated with the ruling classes as to decorate the throne room at Saint James's Palace. Like Trollope and Balzac, both preoccupied with the "cash nexus" of nineteenth-century society, he seems to have been simultaneously attracted and repulsed by the idea of material accretion and its visible sign, luxury. Insisting that he himself would be satisfied with "white-washed walls and plain deal furniture," he could yet advise the Birmingham Society of Arts and School of Design that they could make the desirable simplicity of their house decorations as costly as they pleased: "you may hang your walls with tapestry instead of whitewash or paper; or you may cover them with mosaic, or have them frescoed by a great painter: all this is not luxury, if it be done for beauty's sake, and not for show: it does not break our golden rule: *Have nothing in your houses which you do not*

"Brother Rabbit" chintz by William Morris. (Courtesy of the William Morris Gallery, Walthamstow.)

Sussex rush-bottom armchair by Morris & Co. (Courtesy of the William Morris Gallery, Walthamstow.)

know to be useful or believe to be beautiful." [1] For Morris, the distinction
between beauty, which is good, and luxury, which is bad, lies in the
word *show* and all it implies about the motives and attitudes of
people who employ it.

Morris walked a fine line in many areas of his life. At the height of
his enthusiasm for socialism he saw to it that Morris & Co. operated
at a profit, and the enterprise was, in fact, a model of benevolent
capitalism rather than collectivism, though Morris did work out a
profit-sharing plan with his employees. And yet high prices were not
the result of greed for profits; they were necessary if the firm was to be
able to continue. Morris was fully aware of the complexities of his
situation; as he told Georgiana Burne-Jones: "everyone of us therefore, workman and non-workman, is *forced* to support the present
competitive system by merely living in the present society, and buy-
ing his ordinary daily necessaries: so that an employer by giving up
his individual profit of the goods he gets would not be able to put his
workmen in their proper position: they would be exploited by others
though not by him." [2]

Although Morris was himself extraordinarily learned in all sorts of
abstruse lore, literary and otherwise, particularly in all matters
medieval, and although he wrote a prodigious amount of poetry and
prose (the *Collected Works* runs to twenty-four volumes, plus two
supplementary volumes of writings on art and socialism), he pro-
fessed a disdain for literature as a serious occupation, either in the
reading or writing of it. In *News from Nowhere*, for instance, the
narrator is told that in this ideal England of the future children are
not encouraged to become "book-learned": "You see, children are
mostly given to imitating their elders, and when they see most people
about them engaged in genuinely amusing work, like house-building
and street-paving, and gardening, and the like, that is what they want
to be doing; so I don't think we need fear having too many book-
learned men" (XVI, 31). Morris's poetry, as Henry James observed,
was "only his sub-trade." [3]

His prejudice against book learning dates from his days at Marlborough and Oxford, where he conceived a life-long contempt for the
current aims and methods of public school education. [4] Oxford played

---

[1] Philip Henderson, *William Morris: His Life, Work, and Friends* (New York, 1967), p.
153; "The Beauty of Life," in *The Collected Works of William Morris, with Introductions by
His Daughter May Morris* (1910–15; rpt. New York, 1966), XXII, 77 (italics original). All
quotations from Morris's writings are taken from this edition unless otherwise noted.
As this edition has no lineation, reference is to volume and page.

[2] Henderson, pp. 80 ff., 274. During the late sixties Warington Taylor persuaded
Morris and his friends to charge higher prices than they did at first.

[3] Percy Lubbock, ed., *The Letters of Henry James* (1920; rpt. New York, 1970), I, 17.

[4] J. W. Mackail, *The Life of William Morris* (1899; rpt. New York, 1968), I, 34.

a complex part in Morris's life. Though he detested much that it stood for, it was there that he formed the attachments with Rossetti and Burne-Jones that were to determine to a great extent the course of his life, and some of his feeling for the place is shown in the fervor of his opposition to the proposed restoration, or "vulgarisation," as he termed it, of some of its buildings.[5] Nor were his relationships with Rossetti and Burne-Jones to be stable. We now know that Morris's estrangement from Rossetti must have resulted from Rossetti's passionate attachment to Jane Morris, though their paths would doubtless have diverged eventually in any case. And it is usually inferred from the little evidence surviving that Morris found consolation in a close "friendship" with Georgiana Burne-Jones (who was probably herself in need of consolation because of her own husband's extramarital romantic peccadilloes). Because of zealous discretion by literary executors, however, the emotional truth of these relationships remains obscure; ironically, it is their very obscurity that may be continuing to provoke interest in what, by twentieth-century standards, are rather tame goings-on after all.

At any rate, it is conceivable that Morris's standards were so lofty that Jane Morris, like the original of the several Guinevere portraits for which she posed, thought she "could not breathe in that fine air / That pure severity of perfect light."[6] Or perhaps it was simply difficult to maintain any wifely illusions about a man who punched his own head in frequent fits of temper and excitement. Despite her romantic appearance, she indulged in the most unattractive forms of Victorian hypochondria, which, though fascinating to Rossetti, must have been irritating to her vigorous and energetic husband. A recent biographer, Philip Henderson, conjectures that Morris lacked sympathy for his wife's problems. A close associate, Wilfrid Scawen Blunt, recorded in his diary on the occasion of Morris's death that "he had no thought for anything or person, including himself, but only for the work he had in hand," and that his "life was not arranged in reference" to his wife or to his daughter Jenny, though this outside view is belied by May Morris's recollections of warm family relationships during her childhood (related in her Introductions to the volumes of the *Collected Works*).[7] Even if some of his associates had impressions that Morris lacked consideration for others, he worked diligently throughout his life for the betterment of mankind and probably accomplished more in that direction than most people

[5] See May Morris, ed., *William Morris: Artist, Writer, Socialist* (1936; rpt. New York, 1966), I, 170.

[6] Alfred, Lord Tennyson, "Guinevere," *Idylls of the King*, ll. 640–41.

[7] Henderson, p. 151; Blunt, *My Diaries: Being a Personal Narrative of Events 1888–1914* (1919–20; rpt. New York, 1932), p. 240.

William Morris: *Queen Guinevere*. (Courtesy of The Tate Gallery, London.)

whose personalities radiate warmth and love. The unhappiness of his marriage was not the only source of personal tragedy: his favorite daughter, Jenny, was made an invalid by severe epileptic seizures. Yet Morris in his later years could impress Yeats as the "one perfectly happy and fortunate poet of modern times."[8]

Now that Morris has been dead for over three-quarters of a century, the numerous contradictions of his life have been transmuted into problematic aspects of his reputation. Everyone agrees that Morris exercised a formidable influence in many areas of Victorian life, but it is not yet clear what the results of that influence were. Confusion is rampant in the matter of Morris's place in the evolution of furnishing design; this is perhaps not surprising in view of the fact that the twentieth century, like the nineteenth, is noteworthy for eclecticism rather than homogeneity in its fashions. Despite the one-time prevalence of the so-called Morris chair, for which he is chiefly remembered in America today, Morris did not himself design furniture; all the chairs made by his firm were adaptations of traditional designs found in rural England.[9] Perhaps the most significant effect the Morris firm made on the development of taste in furnishings was the popularization, in fashionable circles, of a certain crudity and naiveté in furniture and decoration; even so, such pseudosimplicity was and is only one of many concurrent fashions.

In the field of textiles and wallpapers, for which Morris personally designed many beautiful patterns, it is now generally agreed among writers on nineteenth-century taste that Morris was not so much an innovator as a brilliant and indefatigable adapter and executor; yet there is still disagreement about the designs he is supposed to have adapted. Peter Floud, for instance, argues that Morris's designs were reactions against the prophetically revolutionary writings and designs of Augustus Pugin and Owen Jones, while Philip Henderson suggests that, while Morris imitated Pugin, it is the interior design work of Wilde, not Morris, that anticipates modern tastes. Ray Watkinson sees Pugin and Jones as precursors of Morris, but "his theoretical ideas were derived, in the first place, from those of the Ecclesiologists, like his master Street; in the second place, from the writings of Ruskin; and from his own experience in the world of

---

[8] William Butler Yeats, "The Happiest of the Poets," *Essays and Introductions* (New York, 1961), p. 54.

[9] About the only similarities between most of the American "Morris chairs" and the ones made by Morris & Co., which inspired them, are the general angularity of shape, the visibility of the wood frames, and, probably the key feature, the mechanism which allows one to adjust the angle of reclining. Most of these derivative chair styles are plainly grotesque and Morris would have loathed them.

Adjustable-back chair by Morris & Co. (Courtesy of the William Morris Gallery, Walthamstow.)

practice, in which the influence of Rossetti, though often oblique, was very strong."[10] The fact is that the whole question of Pugin's influence vis-à-vis that of Ruskin is complex in the extreme, and Morris was doubtless influenced by both in different ways.[11] How far the genesis of Art Nouveau can be attributed to Morris's designs is another point of contention, one that promises to be a long time in its resolution.[12] Perhaps these and other conflicts in opinion will be resolved when we know more about tendencies in nineteenth-century furnishing designs; if we are even yet unable to see in clear perspective these tendencies of a century ago, it is surely fruitless to attempt judgments about Morris's relationship to the design trends of our own era.

Similarly, because the long-range effects of the arts-and-crafts movement have yet to be gauged with any authority, it is difficult to say just how successful was Morris's long struggle to restore individual craftsmanship to the manufacturing process. (He is universally hailed as the inspiration and source of the movement, despite the fact that others took the lead in its instigation; he dragged his feet on the organization of the first exhibition, which nevertheless turned out to be highly successful and was instrumental in directing even greater attention to his work.) Watkinson sees the movement as a focal point out of which came the "fundamental concepts of design for the modern world," but Herbert L. Sussman argues that Morris's "acceptance of the Victorian aesthetic of redundance and naturalism" separates him from those designers who did anticipate modern design by "using the machine to create . . . spare, functional objects." Yet, as Graham Hough points out, it is through the products of industrialization that Morris's influence is felt today:

The people who really bridged the gulf between art and commerce were the plagiarists and imitators, the manufacturers who copied Morris's designs and used them for their machine-made goods. It was Morris's success in the luxury trade that made manufacturers realise that good design was worth having, even in the end worth paying for; and it was the ordinary course of commerce that really distributed the Morris reform in taste throughout the social system. The odd result is that Morris's most lasting and useful effect has been on a kind of production that he himself despised and wanted to abolish.

[10] Floud, "William Morris as an Artist: A New View," *The Listener*, 52 (1954), 562–64; Henderson, p. 206; Watkinson, *William Morris as Designer* (New York, 1967), pp. 30–32; idem, *Pre–Raphaelite Art and Design* (London, 1970), p. 196.
[11] See Kenneth Clark, *The Gothic Revival: An Essay in the History of Taste*, 3rd ed. (1962; rpt. London, 1973), p. 200.
[12] See Henderson, p. 154; Watkinson, *William Morris as Designer*, p. 70; and Geoffrey Warren, *All Colour Book of Art Nouveau* (London, 1972), p. 5.

But this is not quite fair to Morris; in the Utopian society he describes in *News from Nowhere*, machines are useful in freeing men to perform only interesting and fulfilling work. In fact, this is the same state of affairs he envisions in "Art, Wealth, and Riches," where he looks forward "to the invention of machines for performing such labour as is revolting and destructive of self-respect to the men who now have to do it by hand" (XXIII, 160). And Morris & Co. did use machines in circumstances where quality would not be affected. Morris's first consideration was always the achievement of the highest artistic quality; hence the contradiction between the Morris doctrine that there should be no division of labor between designer and craftsman and the actual production practices of Morris & Co., where designs by Morris, Burne-Jones, and others were executed by the firm's employees. Peter Floud, calling attention to this contradiction, argues that Morris's true genius was for designing repeating patterns which

required a type of niggling, mechanical, repetitive handwork altogether different from his picture of the happy medieval stonemason, for example, putting his whole heart into the carving of the capitals in a village church, each one different and expressing his varying moods. . . . This is a strange paradox: that the man whose work, above that of all other designers, was best adapted to that undeviating and infinite multiplication which is the special virtue of the machine should at the same time have been the most eloquent protagonist of hand-crafts as opposed to machine-production.[13]

Perhaps all that can be stated confidently at present is that Morris did succeed in calling attention to the desirability of good design in furniture and textiles. But this is no small achievement.

In the making of stained glass the disparity between Morris's theory and his practice was evident even to the proponents of the arts-and-crafts movement; but the criticism of Morris generated by the movement's having followed his ideas rather than his example was, as A. Charles Sewter points out, "not altogether just" in light of the tremendous achievements of Morris & Co. in an art form that truly lived again in their hands.[14] In fact, the whole idea of the artist-craftsman was so radical in the nineteenth century, when there was a great gulf fixed between "fine" art and the "applied arts," that it would be unrealistic to expect that Morris could immediately have created an entire class of artisans to illustrate his ideal. At that, he carried his idealism so far as to refuse to hire fine cabinetmakers,

---

[13] Watkinson, *William Morris as Designer*, p. 69; Sussman, *Victorians and the Machine: The Literary Response to Technology* (Cambridge, Mass., 1968), pp. 113–22; Hough, *The Last Romantics* (1947; rpt. Oxford, 1961), p. 101; Floud, "The Inconsistencies of William Morris," *The Listener*, 52 (1954), 616.

[14] *The Stained Glass of William Morris and His Circle* (New Haven, 1974), pp. 88–89.

William Morris: "Eve" cartoon for stained glass. (Courtesy of the William Morris Gallery, Walthamstow.)

preferring instead to train his own workmen in order to prove that anyone could become a craftsman (with the result that Morris & Co. furniture is clumsily, even badly, made in comparison with contemporary furniture, both establishment "Victorian" and "medieval-modern".)[15] But for the most part Morris, always sensible within the framework of his idealism, did the best he could with the artists and workers he could find. Like most pioneers, he was ultimately surpassed by his followers, at least with regard to the reintegration of the artistic process into the hands of the artist-craftsman.

Morris devoted much of the time and energy of his later years to the art of printing. Though he did not found the Kelmscott Press until 1890, just six years before his death, it was the fruition of an interest in book design dating back to his early fascination with medieval manuscripts, even before the inception of his plan for publishing *The Earthly Paradise*, for which he and Burne-Jones had engraved a number of wood blocks for the illustrations. Today, as with everything in Morris's life and work, the result of his "little typographical adventure" is a point of disagreement.[16] As with the furniture and textiles produced by the firm, the publications of the Kelmscott Press argued by example for the importance of aesthetic quality in design. Those who prefer to read books rather than to look at them might not choose a Kelmscott Press edition, although it is not difficult to become accustomed to the unfamiliar type; some contemporaries were unsympathetic on the grounds of inferior legibility.[17] A modern critic, Paul Thompson, suggests that the direct influence of Morris's style of book decoration was bad and that his true contribution lies in the impetus his interest in printing as an art gave to a fin de siècle printing revival. Ray Watkinson, on the other hand, sees beneficial effects of Morris's influence on the designs of specific typefaces used subsequently in England and on the Continent.[18] But here again is a paradox: any influence Morris may have had has been realized

---

[15] Clive Wainwright, "English Furniture 1853–1910," Victoria and Albert Museum, London, March 2, 1974.

[16] As Morris described it in a letter to William Bowden asking him to work at the Kelmscott Press, quoted in Watkinson, *William Morris as Designer*, p. 61.

[17] Some unsympathetic American reactions are related by William Dana Orcutt in *Mary Baker Eddy and Her Books* (Boston, 1950), pp. 68–73. Mrs. Eddy objected that the Kelmscott Chaucer was not legible and therefore failed to convey the "beauty of the text"; Charles Eliot Norton was likewise unimpressed and regretted Morris having given a "wrong direction" to the art of printing. In his famous *Theory of the Leisure Class* (1899; new ed. Boston, 1973), Thorstein Veblen cites the productions of the Kelmscott Press as articles good only for "conspicuous consumption," pp. 116–17.

[18] Thompson, *The Work of William Morris* (New York, 1967), pp. 144–45; Watkinson, *William Morris as Designer*, pp. 57–66. See Also John Dreyfus, "William Morris, Typographer," in *William Morris and the Art of the Book* (New York, 1976), pp. 93–94.

Trial page of projected Kelmscott Press edition of *Froissart's Chronicle*. (Courtesy of the William Morris Gallery, Walthamstow.)

through the medium of greater mechanization—his ideal of individual craftsmanship to be expressed in handset type and handmade paper could not withstand the advance of modern printing methods, and so his influence on the improvement of book design resulted in greater attention to the design of mass-produced books.

Although the fact of Morris's socialism is clear, the extent of his commitment to Marxism is another point in dispute. As in the case of other relationships in Morris's life, the course of his love affair with the socialist movement did not run smooth. In 1883 he joined the Democratic Federation, which later became the Social Democratic Federation, and declared himself to be a socialist. His participation was active, but factionalism within the SDF, centered around Henry Myers Hyndman, finally brought about his resignation at the end of 1884. He helped to found the Socialist League in 1885, but after several years of lecturing and joining in socialist demonstrations, the anarchists in the Socialist League made it impossible for Morris to continue. He finally went his own way in 1890, renaming the Hammersmith branch of the league the Hammersmith Socialist Society. Though he became reconciled with the SDF in 1894, he was never again quite so active in the movement. Again, the significance of these events is blurred by the caution and discretion of Morris's literary executors and biographers. The militancy of Morris's views is minimized in Mackail's biography; more recent books, particularly E. P. Thompson's *William Morris: Romantic to Revolutionary*, have stressed the Marxist orthodoxy of his political thinking. But there is no consensus conceding Morris's political development to standard Marxism. James Hulse writes: "The written record certainly does not prove that he was primarily a Marxist; it rather suggests that he was receptive to the ideas of Stepnicek, Kropotkin, and Shaw, in spite of occasional differences and misunderstandings, and that his revolutionary philosophy was not fixed or rigid." Hulse further points out: "It serves little purpose to insist that Morris belonged more to one branch of Socialism, or Communism, or anarchism, than to another. He obviously borrowed fragments of his working Socialism from several sources, and different points of view predominated in his thinking at different times. . . . Morris's Socialism might best be described as catholic, borrowing from the Middle Ages and from Russian nihilism, as well as from Mill and from Marx." [19]

Aside from the question of where Morris got his ideas (in the following chapters I will suggest that they were with him in rudimen-

[19] James W. Hulse, *Revolutionists in London: A Study of Five Unorthodox Socialists* (Oxford, 1970), pp. 109–10.

tary form even from his Oxford days), it is clear to a modern observer that because he advocated a Utopian agrarian society and opposed industrialism, Morris can hardly be considered a true prophet of modern communism, which, after beginning in both Russia and China as "agrarian reform," has in both cases produced rockets and earth satellites as its highest achievements. Philip Henderson attributes the paradoxical aspects of Morris's socialism to his attempt to "wed Ruskin to Marx": "He could hardly be expected to see that after the revolution what he called 'the dull squalor of civilization' would spread even farther. The very last thing people wanted (or want) was to reduce their needs to a minimum in order to achieve Morris's ideal of simplicity of life. In fact, they *liked* all the hideous things produced by the capitalist-controlled machines and wanted ever more of them." And so Morris is today jealously claimed alike by Marxists, and, in the words of Paul Thompson, "anti-Marxist state socialists and anti-socialist simple-lifers with whom he would have had scarcely any sympathy."[20]

The true nature of Morris's influence is, then, very much an open question in the areas of decoration, printing, and politics. His literary reputation is likewise an unsettled matter. Time and scholarship, one hopes, will show that his passing influence on the youthful William Butler Yeats was not his greatest contribution to literature. In the meantime Morris is usually considered a Pre-Raphaelite poet, but this is a misleading classification. For the great bulk of his literary work falls outside any recognized meaning of the term *Pre-Raphaelite* (and the defining of this term is a formidable undertaking in itself). The usual view resulting from the Pre-Raphaelite approach is that, since Morris is a Pre-Raphaelite poet and his later narrative poetry and prose is not noticeably Pre-Raphaelite, these later writings must be bad and are at least superfluous. So W. W. Robson, in his essay "Pre-Raphaelite Poetry," begins his discussion of Morris thus: "William Morris is, in my opinion, much the least interesting of the three poets considered here. What he can do best is illustrated in the early (1858) *Defence of Guenevere* volume, especially the title poem; yet we may find even that poem plaintive and picturesque, rather than rising to the tragic possibilities of its subject; and for the other poems in the volume only a limited compliment seems appropriate, such as that implied when we say they are 'charming.'" Not so condescending is Paul Thompson: "There is no doubt that *The Defence of Guenevere* is by far the most provocative of Morris's books of

---

[20] Henderson, p. 277; see A. L. Morton's Introduction, *Three Works by William Morris* (New York: International Publishers, 1968), pp. 11–32; Thompson, *Work of William Morris*, p. 219.

poems."[21] Even so, such judgments would condemn the other twenty-three volumes of the *Collected Works* to outer darkness forever. A common exercise of Morris critics and biographers is the attempt to define the point at which Morris changed from an early and desirable Pre-Raphaelite style to a flaccid *Earthly Paradise* style and from that to an archaic saga, or northern, style. The irony is that his Pre-Raphaelite style was largely the result of his immaturity and ignorance (or so he later thought), and even the much admired abrupt beginning of "The Defence of Guenevere" is said to have been a felix culpa—the first page of the manuscript having been inadvertently omitted in printing.[22]

But the greatest problem to be resolved with respect to Morris the writer is the apparent irreconcilability of his poetic stance as "the idle singer of an empty day" with the devotion to action he showed in other areas of his life. Robson expresses what is a common opinion about Morris's poetry:

We almost always have the sense in reading Morris's poetry—and indeed his prose romances, too—that what he is doing is quite marginal, quite apart from the main activities of his life. Outside his poetry we know Morris as an energetic, strenuous figure and strong character, the last of the great Victorian "prophets," and more than a "prophet" in being a man of action and a maker. But in his poetry—even after his "Pre-Raphaelite" phase—we observe in an extreme, and a naïve form, the Pre-Raphaelite separation of "art" from "life." "Art" for Morris was essentially a relaxation, an amusement, something to do; writing poetry came easily to him. . . .

What Asa Briggs calls the "deliberately escapist" nature of much of his poetry was responsible, according to Oscar Maurer, Jr., for its popularity with the Victorian reading public—an anomalous situation indeed for an author who said this of his idea of art in an 1882 address:

what I mean by art . . . [is] a general love of beauty, partly for its own sake, and because it is natural and right for the dwellers on the beautiful earth to help and not to mar its beauty, and partly, yes and chiefly, because that external beauty is a symbol of a decent and reasonable life, is above all the token of what chiefly makes life good and not evil, of joy in labour, in creation that is: and this joy in labour, this evidence of man helping in the work of creation, is I feel sure the thing which from the first all progress in civilization has been aiming at: feed this inspiration and you feed the flame of civilization throughout the world; extinguish it, and civilization will die also.[23]

---

[21] Robson, in *The Pelican Guide to English Literature*, Vol. VI, *From Dickens to Hardy* (1958; rpt. Baltimore: Penguin Books, 1964), p. 368; Thompson, *Work of William Morris*, p. 163.

[22] Thompson, *Work of William Morris*, pp. 167–68.

[23] Robson, p. 369; Briggs, Introduction, *William Morris: Selected Writings and Designs*

And so the puzzling inconsistencies and ironies that abound in all other areas of Morris's life and reputation extend to modern critical views of his literary work. It is actually Morris's own deprecatory public posture with regard to his writings that is responsible for this continuing tendency not to take them seriously. While a student at Oxford in 1856, he wrote to a friend: "I can't enter into politico-social subjects with any interest, for on the whole I see that things are in a muddle, and I have no power or vocation to set them right in ever so little a degree. My work is the embodiment of dreams in one form or another."[24] Even while this attitude was echoed by Morris's idle singer of *The Earthly Paradise*, he had repudiated it by becoming involved in an aesthetic revolution with social overtones; later, after having become involved in the most radical political movements of his day, he continued to disavow any serious intent in his writings (except for the obviously politically inspired works, like *A Dream of John Ball*). Even so, there were sporadic attempts to read allegory into such works as *The Wood beyond the World*, but Morris always spurned such suggestions. No doubt Morris's stance was an honest one insofar as his conscious intentions were concerned, but when we go directly to the writings it becomes plain that the poet could not separate himself from the social reformer, for the ideas on which he built his life's work were too basic to his nature to remain unexpressed in his writings, though that expression came indirectly through symbol and association.

Hence it is obvious that serious reappraisal of all Morris's work is needed. Though the questions of his influence in the decorative arts, in printing, and in politics are beyond the scope of this study, in the matter of his "sub-trade," poetry (I use the word in its largest sense), one hopes that careful reading may result in a better understanding of the structure and meaning of the writings themselves. Such reading is, unfortunately, not a common activity; though the prose romances are enjoying a current revival, attributable to the new reading public for fantasy created by the phenomenal popularity of J. R. R. Tolkien's *The Lord of the Rings*, the mature narrative poems are little known today, and when they are read, it is usually in the form of excerpts in anthologies, which cannot, of course, give a sense of the whole. Not surprisingly, they have received only desultory

---

(1962; rpt. Baltimore: Penguin Books, 1968), p. 13; Maurer, "William Morris and the Poetry of Escape," in *Nineteenth Century Studies*, ed. Herbert Davis, William C. DeVane, and R. C. Bald (1940; rpt. New York, 1968), p. 273; "Art: A Serious Thing," in Eugene D. Lemire, ed., *The Unpublished Lectures of William Morris* (Detroit, 1969), pp. 51–52.

[24] Quoted in Mackail, I, 107.

attention from modern critics—our age is not sympathetic to long narrative poems that to many seem like curious but unchallenging fossils. Yet as J. Hillis Miller observes, "All an author's writings form a living unity, just as each individual work is a life within that larger life."[25] If we are ever to understand Morris's work, we must understand it as a "living unity." I have attempted to discover this unity in Morris's most significant poetry and prose fiction.

[25] Miller, *The Disappearance of God: Five Nineteenth-Century Writers* (Cambridge, Mass., 1963), p. viii.

Part One
The Unity of The Earthly Paradise

Introduction to Part One

WITH ITS twenty-four verse tales and double frame story, *The Earthly Paradise* comprises four volumes (originally published as three volumes) and 1,250 pages. With its 42,000 lines of verse, it is four times as long as *Paradise Lost*, three times longer than *The Divine Comedy*, twice the length of its contemporary, *The Ring and the Book*, and twice as long as its model, *The Canterbury Tales*. It is generally regarded as a diffusely written and loosely organized group of unrelated tales. A typical comment is that of Paul Thompson: "The wanderers are purely a device for linking the stories; unlike Chaucer's pilgrims, their precedent, they completely lack individual character, and never affect the style of narrative."[1] This is partially true: the wanderers are not individualized in the way that Chaucer's pilgrims are, and there is no apparent attempt on Morris's part to suit the tales to their narrators' individual personalities. And it is a fact that the separate volumes were published as completed, the individual tales never being reworked in order to make the entire work conform to any carefully controlled pattern, although this is not to say that Morris wrote the tales in the same order in which they appear within the completed scheme. May Morris's introduction to the first volume of *The Earthly Paradise* gives a list of the earliest written tales according to the sequence of some quarto manuscript books, and this listing includes tales from all four volumes of the completed work (see III, xv). The assembly of the tales into volumes does not appear to conform to any careful rationale, however, and one may reasonably expect some shifting in emphasis and point of view in so long a poem. *The Earthly Paradise* does not exhibit the kind of tight construction found in Browning's *Ring and the Book*, nor is its unity as easily perceived as that of Tennyson's *Idylls of the King*, which underwent alterations of already published parts as the whole gradually took shape over a number of years.

Despite the relatively loose organization of *The Earthly Paradise*, however, there are interesting patterns of correspondence between the events of the Prologue and the themes of the tales, patterns that indicate the presence of a delicate network of thematic unity. Far more complex than the overused epithet "escapism" implies, this

[1] *Work of William Morris*, p. 171.

unity is much more profound than the mere awareness of ever-present death which, emanating from every page, no reader can fail to notice. The clue to this unity is not hidden; it is announced in the title of the work.

The phrase "earthly paradise" connotes a vast tradition of thought, originating in antiquity, which has found expression in a multitude of literary works from classical to modern times and which is an aspect of that even greater and more pervasive body of thought that has come, in our day, to be known as primitivism. Arthur O. Lovejoy and George Boas have so expertly delineated the varieties of primitivist theory that a complete recapitulation is as unnecessary as it is impracticable.[2] Generally, the term implies a decline in the condition of mankind since a paradisaical golden age when primeval man lived in harmony with nature and enjoyed, among other delights, that most supreme felicity, eternal life.

By curious twists of human logic, the legend of an Edenic past (to give the concept its Christian perspective) led to the belief that vestiges of this golden age were yet to be found surviving in remote, undiscovered parts of the world.[3] As Henri Baudet, the Dutch social historian, puts it: "The 'noble savage,' unknown to the book of Genesis, was born in that earthly Paradise and seems to have escaped God's attention when Adam and Eve were driven forth, for he remained when the angels with the flaming swords barred our entrance to the Garden of Eden forevermore."[4] By medieval times the earthly paradise, the actuality of which had been argued by Saint Augustine and Saint Thomas Aquinas, had become a theoretically attainable spot, so that Columbus could report to Ferdinand and Isabella in his official account of his third voyage: "I am completely persuaded in my own mind that the Terrestrial Paradise is in the place I have described [referring to the great volume of fresh river water between Trinidad and the South American mainland]."[5] The identification of the golden age of temporal dimension with the earthly paradise of spatial dimension is the key to the basic unity not only of *The Earthly Paradise* but of *The Earthly Paradise* with all Morris's work.

[2] *Primitivism and Related Ideas in Antiquity* (1935; rpt. New York, 1965), pp. 1–22.
[3] See the chart in Harry Levin's *Myth of the Golden Age in the Renaissance* (Bloomington, Ind., 1969), p. 9.
[4] *Paradise on Earth: Some Thoughts on European Images of Non–European Man*, trans. Elizabeth Wentholt (New Haven, 1965), pp. 10–11. See also Lovejoy and Boas, pp. 287–367, and Hoxie Neale Fairchild, *The Noble Savage: A Study in Romantic Naturalism* (New York, 1928), pp. 1–15. A clear and somewhat simplified discussion is contained in A. Bartlett Giamatti, *The Earthly Paradise and the Renaissance Epic* (Princeton, N. J., 1966), pp. 3–33.
[5] Samuel Eliot Morison, ed. and trans., "Letter to the Sovereigns on the Third Voyage, 18 October 1498," *Journals and Other Documents on the Life and Voyages of Christopher Columbus* (New York, 1963), p. 287.

Chapter I

The Apology and Prologue as Overture

The Earthly Paradise begins with "An Apology" in which the narrator, introducing himself as "the idle singer of an empty day," foreshadows the substance of his theme, at once evoking and disclaiming the epic tradition of Virgil, Dante, and Milton:

> Of Heaven or Hell I have no power to sing,
> I cannot ease the burden of your fears,
> Or make quick-coming death a little thing,
> Or bring again the pleasure of past years,
> Nor for my words shall ye forget your tears,
> Or hope again for aught that I can say,
> The idle singer of an empty day.
>
> [III, 1]

What is frankly spelled out in this stanza is demonstrated through the length of The Earthly Paradise. Morris will postulate no after-life—we will read nothing of heaven or hell in the usual sense of these concepts. Those few characters who attain paradisaical bliss within these twenty-four tales will do so on earth, without dying. Translation from the flesh into a spiritual body is not among the hopes of Morris's wanderers, even though they set sail from a Christianized Europe. In fact, one of Morris's recurrent preoccupations in the northern tales is with that most characteristic and familiar of nineteenth-century themes, the passing of paganism, the world "grown grey" from the breath of the "pale Galilean."[1] The contrast between paganism and Christianity is emphasized in the Prologue, as the wanderers' spokesman, Rolf, tells of his attraction to the religion of his ancestors, and forms the subject matter of an important part of the story "The Lovers of Gudrun," in which the Christianization of Iceland results in part from the conversion of the hero Kiartan. In "The Land East of the Sun," John, when questioned by his mother about the heaven promised by the "new faith," replies:

> "Nought know I, mother, of the dead,
> More than thou dost—let be—we live
> This day at least, great joy to give
> Each unto other. . . ."
>
> [V, 67]

[1] Algernon Charles Swinburne, "Hymn to Proserpine," l. 35.

The here and now, not the afterlife promised by Christianity, is Morris's concern not only in *The Earthly Paradise* but throughout his work.

The Apology continues with the first of many references to the heroic pagan substitute for immortality, the cult of fame, which in many literary contexts is referred to metaphorically in terms of the Blessed Isles, or the earthly paradise of heroes in Greek mythology (Valhalla of Germanic mythology is similarly attained only by great warriors):

> So let me sing of names rememberèd,
> Because they, living not, can ne'er be dead,
> Or long time take their memory quite away
> From us poor singers of an empty day.
>
> [III, 1]

In the next stanza the singer disclaims a social message:

> Dreamer of dreams, born out of my due time,
> Why should I strive to set the crooked straight?
> Let it suffice me that my murmuring rhyme
> Beats with light wing against the ivory gate,
> Telling a tale not too importunate
> To those who in the sleepy region stay,
> Lulled by the singer of an empty day.
>
> [III, 1]

Rather, the proclaimed mission of the singer is to

> strive to build a shadowy isle of bliss
> Midmost the beating of the steely sea,
> Where tossed about all hearts of men must be. . . .
>
> [III, 2]

Like the "wizard to a northern king," the singer will cause the drear December wind to be unheard as he creates illusions of spring, summer, and autumn. Thus the present age is likened to winter in the passage of world ages, and the golden spring and summer of the past can be recaptured only through the magic of illusion, or art. The "shadowy isle of bliss" to be created by the singer in his song is the only earthly paradise possible in this December of the world—impossible to be realized even in the autumnal Middle Ages of the wanderers.

In this manner, then, the major themes of *The Earthly Paradise* are foreshadowed, somewhat in the fashion of musical themes in an overture. Because the golden past is dead, because man's life is short and full of trouble, because there is no hope beyond the grave—in short, because there is no paradise, earthly or unearthly—the singer can only beguile us into forgetfulness and into dreams of the dead golden past, the springtime of the world when heroic deeds were still possible, when the crooked could still be set straight. Such is the overt message of the idle singer of the Apology.

Morris amplifies his theme in the Prologue, which opens with a nightmarish vision of the London of his day: "... six counties overhung with smoke, ... the snorting steam and piston stroke, ... the spreading of the hideous town" (III, 3). He evokes this hellish vision only to dismiss it in favor of Chaucer's city, "small and white and clean," its green gardens bordering a clear Thames. But though idyllic, the London of Chaucer is far from Edenic—it is to serve only as an emblem of the fourteenth century, the time of the wanderers. Morris, despite his disclaimers in the voice of the idle singer as to didactic social intentions, seems to be a *laudator temporis acti* more extreme than Carlyle in *Past and Present*, for Morris's superior model is not the medieval system (despite his famous "medievalism"), but the primitive and pagan heroic culture that preceded the Christian Middle Ages. The wanderers are to leave their medieval homes to search for a more remote and unattainable golden past, to be realized in the earthly paradise of their destination, a paradise not to be understood in terms of the Christian church's teachings about immortality.

The "nameless city" to which the narrator directs attention is the home of descendants of Greek wanderers of a more distant time. In this city of "marble palaces" and "pillared council-house," "Thronged with much people clad in ancient guise," the culture of the inhabitants' Ionian forebears is preserved. So, in the twilight of their own culture, the northern wanderers succeed only in finding a vestige of a culture already dead. It is the pattern of the Prologue that the search for unending life inevitably results in an encounter with a memento mori. Rolf's history, as told to the elders of the city, illustrates the deterioration of northern culture. Although born a Christian in Byzantium, he had learned in youth the stories of Norse mythology and, on visiting his ancestral home, had been struck by the contrast between the harsh realities of northern life and his childhood dreams of Asgard:

> But when I reached one dying autumn-tide
> My uncle's dwelling near the forest side,
> And saw the land so scanty and so bare,
> And all the hard things men contend with there,
> A little and unworthy land it seemed,

And all the more of Asgard's days I dreamed,
And worthier seemed the ancient faith of praise.

[III, 6]

The "autumn-tide" of his visit metaphorically underscores the state
of decay of northern culture in the fourteenth century as contrasted
with its heroic legendary springtime. The balance Morris sets up
between the vestigial Greek culture of the nameless host city and the
attenuated northern, or Germanic, culture represented by the various wanderers is a telling comment upon the nature of civilization in
general and Western Europe in particular, regardless of the singer's
earlier denials of social comment. Elsewhere Morris would compare
"the Great Story of the North," as he termed the *Volsunga Saga* (thus
showing the intensity of his heart's affection), to the "Tale of Troy" in
its significance for posterity (VII, 286); the juxtaposition of these two
cultures, Germanic and Greek, is integral to Morris's primitivist
major theme in *The Earthly Paradise*: the alternation between stories
of Greek and northern legend represents in symbolic fashion his idea
of the parallelism of these two cultures. Oswald Spengler, many years
later, in synthesizing the anthropology and mythology of the Cambridge School and others, formulated his "contemporary and
spiritual epochs" which he charted for Indian, Classical, Arabian,
and Western civilizations in periods designated "Spring" through
"Winter."[2] He was widely regarded as a prophet in his own day but is
now, except in one important sense, a prophet without honor. But the
truth of poetry is not the truth of history nor the truth of science; what
remains valid in Spengler's lucubration is the truth of poetry, and this
truth is almost precisely (or is in every way analogous) to Morris's
"truth" in these tales. Morris believed himself to be living near the
final collapse of the civilization of the north, that is, of Western
Europe, a demise that would repeat that of the already dead Greek
civilization. The widespread Aryan fever of the nineteenth century
had its effect on Morris, whose enthusiasm for Icelandic subjects led
him to abandon wife, children, home, and friends for months on end,
but he was always able to view the civilization of the north with a
certain amount of objectivity, an objectivity that places Morris in the
vanguard of nineteenth-century thinkers on mythology and anthropology.

Rolf's dreams of Asgard were mingled with the ancient legends of
the earthly paradise, "gardens ever blossoming / Across the western
sea where none grew old" (III, 7), told him by the Breton squire

---

[2] *The Decline of the West*, Vol. I, *Form and Actuality*, trans. Charles Francis Atkinson
(1926; rpt. New York, 1947), following p. 428.

Nicholas. Now, Rolf's longing for the golden past is identified with
the quest for the earthly paradise, the vestigial golden age of man's
infancy. These two concepts of immortality—the golden days of Asgard and the Blessed Isles of legend—are supplemented by a third
concept, the alchemist's search for the elixir of immortality, or fountain of youth, carried on by Laurence, the Swabian priest. The fountain of youth is frequently associated with the terrestrial paradises of
legend and literature, and Sabine Baring-Gould, the clergyman
turned novelist and mythographer, makes much of it in a fine collection that was widely known in its day.[3] Laurence is fascinated with
stories of vanished earthly heroes who live yet and will return:

> Tales of the Kaiser Redbeard could he tell
> Who neither went to Heaven nor yet to Hell,
> When from that fight upon the Asian plain
> He vanished, but still lives to come again
> Men know not how or when; but I listening
> Unto this tale thought it a certain thing
> That in some hidden vale of Swithiod
> Across the golden pavement still he trod.
>
> [III, 8]

The motif of the returning hero, to be stressed in "Ogier the Dane,"
which is based upon the legends clustering around Charlemagne and
his knights, suggests other parallels in legend and myth. The expected return of King Arthur is an obvious analogue; a more spectacular one is the prophesied Second Coming of Jesus Christ, an event
that is to coincide with the world cataclysm ushering in the millennium, that is, the new heaven and the new earth of Revelation,
when death will be overcome and eternity will conquer time. (The
Judeo-Christian idea is that time will come to an end, whereas the
classical pagan conception is that the apocalypse is followed by a new
paradisaical period.)[4] The reference to the tales of heroes told by
Laurence, then, is the first hint of the relationship between the hero
and the renewal of society and the rebirth of the world itself into a
new cycle of ages. This relationship is to form a basic pattern within
the tales of *The Earthly Paradise*, as well as in Morris's other writings.

It is on a "bright September afternoon" (III,8), the autumn weather
corresponding to the autumnal lengthening shadows of their
fourteenth-century civilization, that these three, Rolf, Nicholas, and
Laurence, decide to leave their pestilence-ridden home in search of

---

[3] *Curious Myths of the Middle Ages* (1867; rpt. New Hyde Park, N. Y., 1967), pp. 250–65.
[4] See Mircea Eliade, *The Myth of the Eternal Return*, trans. Willard R. Trask (New
York, 1954), pp. 126–30, and M. H. Abrams, *Natural Supernaturalism: Tradition and
Revolution in Romantic Literature* (New York, 1971), pp. 34–37.

the earthly paradise (recalling the dusk into which the aged Ulysses and his mariners sail in Tennyson's poem). Nicholas, making the suggestion, invites his friends to

> go with me to-night,
> Setting your faces to undreamed delight,
> Turning your backs unto this troublous hell. . . .
>
> [III, 9]

This is the only hell to be found in the pages of *The Earthly Paradise*— the hard life of mortals in the world of reality. In "The Watching of the Falcon" Morris suggests that only the gift of death keeps this world from becoming a hell (IV, 161–62). The implication is, then, that eternal life per se is not enough—the world must be changed, or renewed.

Continuing his history, Rolf tells of the encounter with the English king Edward III. Although he is not identified by name, there is, in the first discarded version of the Prologue, a note calling for an illustration of "Edward on his galley at Sluse" (XXIV, 95). Edward, victorious against the French in the naval battle off Sluis, was later forced to vitiate his triumph by making a truce. Thus the aging king, surrounded by the trappings of heroic martial feats, is emblematic of the crepuscular civilization of which he is the epitome—a society in which heroic virtues have limited power. Morris presents Edward as the prototype of the noble leader who governs his people wisely and honorably but is approaching the twilight of his life and reign (though the historical Edward was at the time of Sluis actually only a little more than halfway through his reign):

> Broad-browed he was, hook-nosed, with wide grey eyes
> No longer eager for the coming prize,
> But keen and steadfast; many an ageing line,
> Half hidden by his sweeping beard and fine,
> Ploughed his thin cheeks, his hair was more than grey,
> And like to one he seemed whose better day
> Is over to himself, though foolish fame
> Shouts louder year by year his empty name.
>
> [III, 16]

Nevertheless, the principle of heroic leadership that Edward III represents is still valid—we shall see that one of Morris's major concerns in *The Earthly Paradise* is the necessity for such leadership and its inherent problems—and dreams of heroic death are awakened in Rolf by the stirring challenge of the king to follow him:

> Ah, with such an one
> Could I from town to town of France have run

> To end my life upon some glorious day
> Where stand the banners brighter than the May
> Above the deeds of men, as certainly
> This king himself has full oft wished to die.
>
> [III, 15]

Either to follow or to oppose such a king would be glorious:

> Nor had it been an evil lot to stand
> On the worse side, with people of the land
> 'Gainst such a man, when even this might fall,
> That it might be my luck some day to call
> My battle-cry o'er his low-lying head,
> And I be evermore rememberèd.
>
> [III,15]

Nicholas, fearing Rolf's acceptance of the king's invitation to follow him, explains their mission and elicits a rueful response from the king:

> "For you the world is wide—but not for me,
> Who once had dreams of one great victory
> Wherein that world lay vanquished by my throne,
> And now, the victor in so many an one,
> Find that in Asia Alexander died
> And will not live again; . . .
>
> . . . . .
>
> "Farewell, it yet may hap that I a king
> Shall be remembered but by this one thing,
> That on the morn before ye crossed the sea
> Ye gave and took in common talk with me."
>
> [III, 20–21]

Thus all the pagan concepts of immortality are introduced in the Prologue: Asgard, the earthly paradise or Blessed Isles, the elixir of life, the cult of fame. But the wanderers will be granted only visions of death, and that soon.

Upon finding land, which we may assume is somewhere in Central America, the wanderers are delirious with joy, thinking that they have "reached the gates of Paradise / And endless bliss" (III, 28). (The equating of the Americas with the earthly paradise has historical authority, as may be inferred from our earlier quotation from Christopher Columbus.[5] The plausible historicity of the events of the Prologue is an important point, and we shall return to it later.) Following a pathway up a hill, they find a monstrous burial place of kings:

[5] On this point see Baudet, pp. 26 ff., Giamatti, p. 4, and Abrams, pp. 411–12.

> And there a rude shrine stood, of unhewn stones
> Both walls and roof, with a great heap of bones
> Piled up outside it. . . .
>
> [III, 32]

Inside the shrine is a golden idol, and hanging on the walls are the corpses of dead kings. On the mountain's summit is yet another grisly tableau, the meaning of which is not completely explained until much later: clad like his predecessors within the shrine, a dying king lies on the rocky ground surrounded by embalmed corpses "Set up like players at a yule-tide feast" (III, 33), depicting various stations of life. These dread reminders of death-in-life, ironically juxtaposed with the wanderers' meeting with Edward III, illustrate the futility of human striving in a world where even kings must die.

Forcibly wrenched into awareness that this cannot be the land of immortality, the wanderers are nonetheless favorably impressed with the inhabitants of this forest community:

> And sure of all the folk I ever saw
> These were the gentlest: if they had a law
> We knew not then, but still they seemed to be
> Like the gold people of antiquity.
>
> [III, 37]

These noble savages live in a vestigial Bronze Age culture:

> But nought of iron did they seem to know,
> For all their cutting tools were edged with flint,
> Or with soft copper, that soon turned and bent. . . .
>
> [III, 37]

These handsome people, "comely and well knit," clad in their cotton or woven garments with ornaments of beaten gold, represent an earlier and more primitive, hence more admirable, level of culture. Ironically, when asked about the whereabouts of the "good land," these aborigines point eastward, and, told that the wanderers had come from the east, they kneel down to worship their more "civilized" visitors. Conversely, the wanderers are infused with new hope by finding the simpler bronze culture, as if, so much of the past being found still alive, the age of gold might yet exist:

> But we, though somewhat troubled at this thing,
> Failed not to hope, because it seemed to us
> That this so simple folk and virtuous,
> So happy midst their dreary forest bowers,
> Showed at the least a better land than ours,
> And some yet better thing far onward lay.
>
> [III, 37]

But though their quest will take them further into barbarity and bestiality—the heart of darkness—the wanderers will never gain the paradisaical past they seek. From this point Rolf is haunted by dreams as well as by actual experiences of death and decay: at the next landing site Rolf is wakened from a dream of love and death by an attack of wild men (III, 40–41). The dream is prophetic: Kirstin, the beloved of Nicholas, is killed in the fighting.

Several fruitless encounters with the wild people are followed by another landing, and the experience of the wanderers at this place recalls the earlier visit with the Bronze Age forest folk. These naked brown people are even more primitive, "most untaught and wild, / Nigh void of arts, but harmless, good and mild" (III, 44). When they are questioned as to the location of the earthly paradise, they tell of the land beyond the mountains:

> Beyond them lay a fair abode of bliss
> Where dwelt men like the Gods, and clad as we,
> Who doubtless lived on through eternity
> Unless the very world should come to nought;
> But never had they had the impious thought
> To scale those mountains; since most surely, none
> Of men they knew could follow up the sun,
> The fearful sun, and live; but as for us
> They said, who were so wise and glorious
> It might not be so.
>
> [III, 45]

This passage underscores one of the central ironies of the Prologue: the Promethean aspects of the northern civilization represented by Rolf and the other wanderers have been turned to regressive aims, their quest essentially denying the validity of the civilization this Prometheanism has produced, while the simpler, acquiescent cultures with which the wanderers come in contact consistently regard their visitors as godlike because of their superior technology. Rolf's speech rousing his companions to conquer the mountains illustrates the basic paradox of their quest to find a land where quests will be unnecessary:

> "Did ye then deem the way would not be rough
> Unto the lovely land ye so desire?
>
> . . . . .
>
> "Lo now, if but the half will come with me,
> The summit of those mountains will I see,
> Or else die first; . . .
>
> . . . . .
>
> . . . alone, O friends, will I

> Seek for my life, for no man can die twice,
> And death or life may give me Paradise! "
>
> [III, 46–47]

The chastening of the Promethean spirit that is implicit in the story of the wanderers recurs often in the verse tales: the legend of the rebellious fire-bringer, associated since its earliest version in Hesiod with the end of the golden age, implies faith in progress, a concept inimical to primitivism.[6]

, By this time some of the wanderers have already learned their lesson—"yet are we grown too wise / Upon this earth to seek for Paradise" (III, 47–48)—and they choose to remain behind. Their renunciation of the quest will be repeated by others and is shown to be justified by the outcome of the expedition to brave the mountains. Rolf and his diminished band of followers suffer greatly and, in the end, find only a land of cannibals. The series of cultures found by the wanderers illustrates a return to primitivism, but a primitivism unacceptable to the wanderers' preconceived ideals. This cultural retrogression is echoed in their own natures: in their quest for the happy land they become increasingly brutalized, mercilessly killing prisoners taken in skirmishes with the wild men: "So with the failing of our hoped delight / We grew to be like devils" (III, 49). Once again, death being found where life is sought, the wanderers are themselves participants in death.

Next, in a respite from their struggle, they dwell for a number of years as honored guests in a beautiful city inhabited by a people kin to the forest dwellers, also a Bronze Age culture:

> Their arms were edged with copper or with gold,
> Whereof they had great plenty, or with flint;
> No armour had they fit to bear the dint
> Of tools like ours, and little could avail
> Their archer craft; their boats knew nought of sail,
> And many a feat of building could we show,
> Which midst their splendour still they did not know.
>
> [III, 58]

The wanderers, with their superior military skill, deliver their hosts from the persecutions of a tyrant conqueror who periodically demands human tribute for sacrifice, a motif prefiguring a number of tales in *The Earthly Paradise*. Though tempted to remain amid their grateful hosts, Rolf and Nicholas are not yet resigned to the failure of their quest and so push on to the conclusion of their hopes:

[6] See Lovejoy and Boas, pp. 196–99; Abrams, pp. 56–65, discusses the relationship of the idea of progress to Judeo-Christian millennial concepts.

And we had lived and died as happy there
As any men the labouring earth may bear,
But for the poison of that wickedness
That led us on God's edicts to redress.

[III, 59]

A bitterly ironic episode ends this history. Dupes of a young man pretending to lead them to the land of immortality, the wanderers are kept as captive gods and treated to a final and most horrifying spectacle of death:

Bound did we sit, each in his golden chair,
Beholding many mummeries that they wrought
About the altar; till at last they brought,
Crowned with fair flowers, and clad in robes of gold,
The folk that from the wood we won of old.
Why make long words? before our very eyes
Our friends they slew, a fitting sacrifice
To us their new-gained Gods, who sought to find
Within that land, a people just and kind
That could not die, or take away the breath
From living men.

[III, 73]

While the city is under attack, the wanderers succeed in escaping. Though their erstwhile captors regard them as potential saviors, they are pleased to see the downfall of their worshipers as they desert the city and, for the last time, take to the sea. This episode is the most cynical comment upon the nature of religion in all *The Earthly Paradise*; its impact is reinforced in the verse tales by repeated rescues from religious sacrifice and the generally capricious nature of the gods depicted by Morris.

The story of the wanderers is the characteristic epic voyage in reverse. Odysseus returns to Ithaca and Penelope after a great war still accomplishing great deeds, killing the usurpers and reestablishing his own sovereignty; Aeneas similarly carves a heroic path to his new home, slaughtering with godlike mercilessness the enemies of the divinely ordained Rome. But these wanderers desert their homes, rejecting heroism and the immortality of fame in hope of earthly immortality in a land where striving ceases. Their quest is psychologically regressive: their wish to find paradise, or the golden age of man, is, on the psychological level, an attempt to return to a state of infancy, or sensual gratification without attendant anxiety or care. By contrast, Tolstoy's Ivan Ilyitch achieves salvation by regression to a state of infancy, but the authorial outlook is Christian, not pagan: Tolstoy's protagonist must, through his illness, become as a little child before he can be saved from the mindless triviality of his bourgeois existence. But the wanderers, like Tennyson's mariners tempted in the land of the lotos-eaters, want "long rest or death, dark death, or dreamful ease." Except for those who stay behind with the brown-skinned people, the wanderers do not establish a new home, but find only a series of temporary havens, their final hosts being the elders of the nameless city. There, the wanderers have no thought of taking wives and founding families—another aspect of their mortality, for their flesh will not even have biological continuity with future beings. As in Tennyson's "Ulysses," where the same curious mixture of Victorian Prometheanism and regressive death wish results in a last quest for the "Happy Isles," the journey's end for the wanderers is in fact seen to be a voyage to the end of night.[7]

On the other hand, the wanderers represent a warrior culture, though a decrepit one, as constant references to their superior weapons and military prowess emphasize, and the turning away from deeds by these "children of a warrior race" (III, 74) implies that heroism is not possible in this fourteenth-century twilight of the northern race. Now they can only thrill to stories of deeds done long before the earth (and they themselves) grew old:

> many things like these
> They talked about, till they seemed young again,
> Remembering what a glory and a gain
> Their fathers deemed the death of kings to be.
>
> · · · · ·
>
> The minstrels raised some high heroic strain
> That led men on to battle in old times;
> And midst the glory of its mingling rhymes,
> Their hard hearts softened, and strange thoughts arose
> Of some new end to all life's cruel foes.
>
> [III, 266]

The implication of the Prologue is that the wanderers should have been content to remain with the Bronze Age cultures with which they first came in contact. Retrogression to a heroic age, in which great deeds could be done by great men, before commercialism had sullied pagan virtues, is as far back as man can travel. Such a concept is in accord with the heroic subject matter of most of Morris's writings. The wanderers are now able to experience deeds of heroism only vicariously, through art, and the stories they tell, as they are remembered and retold, will constitute their only immortality. Their aged condition metaphorically represents the world grown old, while the

[7]"The Lotos-Eaters," l. 98, and "Ulysses," l. 63.

young people with whom they are surrounded, and the young heroes and heroines of their stories, represent the young world of long ago. Their deeds are now the subject of tales told in an old world where deeds are no longer possible.

The age of the wanderers, now old and withered, is contrasted with youth in the links that separate the tales. For instance:

> And now the watery April sun lit up
> Upon the fair board golden ewer and cup,
> And over the bright silken tapestry
> The fresh young boughs were gladdening every eye,
> And round the board old faces you might see
> Amidst the blossoms and their greenery.
>
> [III, 170]

Or:

> Then round about the grave old men they drew,
> Both youths and maidens; and beneath their feet
> The grass seemed greener and the flowers more sweet
> Unto the elders, as they stood around.
>
> [IV, 126]

The descriptions of the pastoral activities of the young people of the nameless city give a sense of what the wanderers have lost through their fruitless quest:

> Neath the bright sky cool grew the weary earth,
> And many a bud in that fair hour had birth
> Upon the garden bushes; in the west
> The sky got ready for the great sun's rest,
> And all was fresh and lovely; none the less,
> Although those old men shared the happiness
> Of the bright eve, 'twas mixed with memories
> Of how they might in old times have been wise,
> Not casting by for very wilfulness
> What wealth might come their changing life to bless;
> Lulling their hearts to sleep, amid the cold
> Of bitter times, that so they might behold
> Some joy at last, e'en if it lingered long;
> That, wearing not their souls with grief and wrong,
> They still might watch the changing world go by,
> Content to live, content at last to die.
> Alas! if they had reached content at last,
> It was perforce when all their strength was past;
> And after loss of many days once bright,
> With foolish hopes of unattained delight.
>
> [IV, 186]

By seeking the phantasmal earthly paradise, they have paradoxically lost the only happiness possible to man in a real world—a simple life in accord with nature's rhythms. This natural state, the only Edenic state possible, has been lost through Promethean disobedience, refusal to accept the limitations of mortality. The pattern of the wanderers' lives is the pattern of the Fall; the pattern of redemption is found in the verse tales that follow the Prologue.

Chapter II

The Role of the Hero

THE TRANSITION FROM the world of the Prologue to that of the verse tales shifts us abruptly from realism to fantasy. While the events of the Prologue have historical antecedents, the provenances of the tales are folktale, legend, and saga. (A possible exception is "The Lovers of Gudrun," the source for which, *The Laxdoela Saga*, had a spurious reputation for historicity, a point to be discussed later.) The cities and nations mentioned in the Prologue are real, Edward III is a historical figure, and the voyage itself is based on actual expeditions; the outcome of the voyage is inevitable in this realistic context. (That this contrast is deliberate and the result of much consideration on Morris's part is shown by his discarding of the first prologue, "The Wanderers," which impinges on fantasy.) The wanderers have mistaken art for reality and must fail. Nevertheless, there is an essential relationship between art and life, and it is this relationship that is explored in the verse tales.

With "The Man Born to Be King," the second tale for March, Morris introduces the major concern of the tales (as it is of many of his writings)—that of the hero-king who is fated to be the great leader and savior of his people. Michael, the protagonist of this tale, is not a culture hero in the same sense as Perseus, Theseus, Sigurd, and Arthur, but the tale itself shows a relationship with the typical pattern of the life of the culture hero. (I use the term to mean "a mythical or mythicized historical figure who embodies the aspirations or ideals of a society.")[1] The humble birth, the prophesied greatness, the attempted murder of the newborn child by a jealous king are all standard incidents in the widespread folktale type of which this particular story is representative, but they are probably best known in the West as they appear in the New Testament account of the birth of Jesus.[2] These elements also appear in somewhat attenuated form in the account in Genesis of the childhood of Moses, and any or all of them may be detected in the histories of the great culture heroes

[1] *Random House Dictionary of the English Language* (New York, 1966), s.v. culture hero.
[2] Tale Type 930 in Stith Thompson's *Types of the Folktale*, FF Communications, Vol. 75, No. 184 (Helsinki, 1964), pp. 325–26.

already mentioned. Additionally, this pattern of motifs is related to the legendary biographies attributed to kings by their chroniclers throughout history.[3] The point for readers of Morris is that this simple and unpretentious tale touches upon a massive complex of related myths, legends, and folktales that associate the heroic and usually semidivine leader with the bringing in of the millennium, or the return of the golden age.[4] The mystical relationship of the hero or leader to society is stressed throughout *The Earthly Paradise* and is brought out clearly in the low-keyed märchen atmosphere of "The Man Born to Be King."

The importance of appropriate leadership is emphasized in the opening lines:

> A king there was in days of old
> Who ruled wide lands, nor lacked for gold,
> Nor honour, nor much longed-for praise,
> And his days were called happy days,
> So peaceable his kingdoms were,
> While others wrapt in war and fear
> Fell ever unto worse and worse.
>
> [III, 107]

This king, though a good ruler by Machiavellian standards, is guilty of hubris and, like Arnold's Mycerinus, must learn to subordinate his will to the ineluctable workings of destiny. His attempts to avert what is written in the stars must, like those of Oedipus, fail, and he comes at length to repent his Promethean pride as he relinquishes his throne to Michael, the "man born to be king":

> "How many an hour might I have been
> Right merry in the gardens green;
> How many a glorious day had I
> Made happy with some victory;
> What noble deeds I might have done,
> What bright renown my deeds have won;
> What blessings would have made me glad;
> What little burdens had I had,
> What calmness in the hope of praise,

---

[3] Joseph Campbell discusses the biography of Sargon and its affinities with that of Moses, Romulus and Remus, and others in *The Masks of God: Occidental Mythology* (New York, 1964), pp. 72 ff. See also Lord Raglan, *The Hero: A Study in Tradition, Myth, and Drama* (1956; rpt. Westport, Conn., 1975), for an extended analysis of the lives of heroes.

[4] On the subject of Virgil's "prophecies" and the reign of Augustus as a golden age, see Campbell's *Masks of God: Occidental Mythology*, pp. 322–34. He discusses also the Jewish concepts of apocalypse and the messiah, pp. 269–71.

> What joy of well-accomplished days,
> If I had let these things alone;
> Nor sought to sit upon my throne
> Like God between the cherubim."
>
> [III, 166–67]

The second tale for April, "The Proud King," concerns exclusively the chastening of a leader who "thought that he was something more than man, if not equal to God" (III, 242, "The Argument"). One of the forms of this king's inordinate egocentricity is a conviction that he is immortal: "Still I may not die / Though underneath the earth my fathers lie" (III, 243). Through his suffering he gains a conviction of his own infinitesimal part in God's plan. Although this tale is basically Christian not only in setting but in its moral point, its emphasis on the need for acquiescence in the cosmic scheme is consonant with the pagan heroic stories of *The Earthly Paradise*. In each of the tales the fated pattern of human events is as inexorable as the progression of seasons to which, in fact, human change is constantly likened. For instance, the accession of Michael is described as follows:

> And straight the autumn air did burn
> With many a point of steel and gold;
> And through the trees the carol rolled
> Once more, until the autumn thrush
> Far off 'gan twittering on his bush,
> Made mindful of the long-lived spring.
>
> [III, 167]

The new reign is a new beginning of time, a spring following the autumnal decline and abdication of the old king, a renewal of the age of gold when greed is unknown and peace covers the earth:

> Nor will the poor folk see again
> A king like him on any throne,
> Or such good deeds to all men done:
> For then, as saith the chronicle,
> It was the time, as all men tell,
> When scarce a man would stop to gaze
> At gold crowns hung above the ways.
>
> [III, 167]

The theme of the chastening of Promethean efforts to avert fate is immediately repeated by Morris in the first tale for April, "The Doom of King Acrisius." Morris underscores this theme with his choice of title, for the story is, of course, that of Perseus. His jealous grandfather, King Acrisius, is a relatively minor character. The paradoxical bringing about of events through efforts to avoid them echoes the ironic results of the wanderers' expedition:

> Now of the King Acrisius shall ye hear,
> Who, thinking he could free his life from fear,
> Did that which brought but death on him at last.
>
> [III, 171]

Acrisius' futile efforts to thwart the destined greatness of his daughter's son fall into the pattern of the traditional difficulties of birth of the culture hero, as already touched upon in "The Man Born to Be King." Perseus is the first of the great legendary heroes to appear in *The Earthly Paradise*, and his exploits illustrate well the relationship of the culture hero to the society he represents.[5] Fated, like Oedipus, to bring destruction to his own family in the person of Acrisius, he bears what in Greek legend is analogous to the mark of Cain, a symbolic guilt resulting from Original Sin, a concept always associated with the myth of the Fall. We shall see that the Cain motif is amplified by Morris in a number of subsequent tales. (The Cain motif is implied, rather than explicit, in "The Man Born to Be King"; Michael's supplanting of the king presupposes some sort of symbolic death of the old king.) The significance of the hero's fated guilt is this: the culture hero typically embodies, represents, or brings about not only the salvation of his society but its collective and inevitable inheritance of guilt as well, and it is this guilt, at once his own and that of his people, that must be purged and atoned for in the heroic endeavors he is fated to play out. Perseus' most striking adventure, the battle with the sea monster to which Andromeda is a sacrifice, is a classic act of heroism and one that emblematizes his role as savior. The reward of the hero may be only suffering (as in the case of Jesus and of Oedipus), fame and honor (as with Perseus and Bellerophon), or both (as with Sigurd); but he will, no matter what, be the instrument of his society's rebirth.

In Christian terms the hero's life may be understood as elliptically representing the pattern of mankind's fall from grace and redemption through the atonement of the savior Jesus; in the terms of the classical writers, the hero's life is a paradigm of the loss of the golden age and its restoration. (The ontology implied is cyclical; such a view of history is consonant with certain types of primitivist thought: a gradual deterioration may be effected through a series of cyclical movements of decline and rebirth.)[6] So Perseus, purified of his guilt,

---

[5] See ibid., pp. 128–29, for a provocative comparison between Moses and Perseus; both of these hero-figures are included in Lord Raglan's analysis, pp. 173 ff.

[6] See Lovejoy and Boas, p. 3.

becomes the founder of a city, Mycenae, and institutes there a reign of peace and prosperity—a symbolic re-creation of the golden age— recalling the reign of Michael in "The Man Born to Be King":

> Peaceful grew the land
> The while the ivory rod was in his hand,
> For robbers fled, and good men still waxed strong,
> And in no house was any sound of wrong,
> Until the Golden Age seemed there to be,
> So steeped the land was in felicity.
>
> [III, 238]

The role enacted by the hero is foreordained, a fact demonstrated in the prophecies of his deeds of greatness, and cannot be circumvented by external events. His heroism lies in the willingness of the hero to undergo his appointed ordeal. He must submit himself to his fate, whatever it may be, even if, as in the case of Jesus, of Sigurd, of Browning's Childe Roland, and, for that matter, Oliver in Morris's own early short poem "The Tune of Seven Towers," he has foreknowledge of a tragic end. Hence the insistence on the inevitability of fate in the tales of *The Earthly Paradise*.

If, on the other hand, the hero should refuse the call to action, he becomes a victim, doomed to ignominious disintegration.[7] This is illustrated in the second tale for June, "The Lady of the Land." Having failed through fear to kiss and thereby disenchant the lady-dragon, the Italian mariner suffers horribly before dying. The effect of this tale upon the listeners in the nameless Greek city is twofold: the young men feel contempt, the old compassion. The latter remember

> well how fear in days gone by
> Had dealt with them and poisoned wretchedly
> Good days, good deeds and longings for all good. . . .
>
> [IV, 142]

Thus the hero carries upon his shoulders the responsibility for accomplishing his destiny—herein lies his courage, which must not be confused with mere egoism. Although Morris's heroes are proud, their pride, the product of a mystical apprehension of their preordained roles, is subordinate to the symbolic importance of the role, as opposed to their individual worth.

"The Story of Rhodope" and "The Fostering of Aslaug" illustrate the inscrutable workings of fate in the lives of girls destined to

---

[7] Joseph Campbell interprets the hero's refusal as "essentially a refusal to give up what one takes to be one's own interest" (*The Hero with a Thousand Faces*, 2d ed. [Princeton, N.J., 1968], pp. 59–60).

become queens. Significantly different in detail and source, they are yet both recognizable analogues to the tale best known as "Cinderella." Rhodope's unusual destiny is hinted in the dream of her father preceding her birth, in which a tiny blossom grows into a tree hung with omens of her future:

> on each bough did hang
> Crown, sword, or ship, or temple fair to see;
> And therewithal a great wind through it sang,
> And trumpet blast there was; and armour rang
> Amid that leafy world. . . .
>
> [V, 211]

The preternatural and unfathomable actions of the eagle tend to make the events of the tale seem inevitable; by contrast, in the famous Perrault version of the story, the supernatural helper, appearing as a somewhat capricious fairy godmother, lends no sense of ineluctable destiny to the tale but is, rather, the agency by which virtue is rewarded. Typically, for Morris, the sense of fate is emphasized, as, for instance, when Rhodope's father speaks: "Fate shall yet prevail, / Though oft we deem we lead her thereunto" (V, 235).   In "The Fostering of Aslaug" the heroine's heritage of royalty as the child of Sigurd and Brynhild is the factor that cannot be nullified by the base machinations of her villainous foster parents. (The bringing up of the royal child by humble foster parents is one of the standard features of the traditional king's biography already alluded to.)[8] This austere northern tale is devoid of supernatural devices and omens, and its atmosphere of inevitability depends upon the girl's inborn conviction of her destiny, despite the mean servitude she is forced to undergo:

> "I was not made for misery.
>
>   .   .   .   .   .
>
>   . . . who knows
> But I am kept for greater woes,
> Godlike despair that makes not base. . . . "
>
> [VI, 40]

Her sense of her own superiority to her circumstances, expressed paradoxically in her perfect obedience and voluntary dumbness, is recognized by her vicious mistress, whose fear of Aslaug's "awful beauty" (VI, 37) prevents her from killing the girl. The destined union of Aslaug with Ragnar is marked by their separate dream visions of Sigurd and Brynhild, expressing their felicity at the marriage which will rejuvenate the earth. In Ragnar's vision, in which Sigurd and

---

[8] See Campbell, *Masks of God: Occidental Mythology,* pp. 73 ff.

Brynhild are seen through a wall of flame (an interesting treatment of the otherworld, which will concern us later), he is given a lily by Sigurd which, set in the earth, fructifies the wasteland:

> "Great light upon the world did fall,
> And fair the sun rose o'er the earth,
> And blithe I grew and full of mirth:
> And no more on a waste I was,
> But in a green world, where the grass
> White lily-blooms well-nigh did hide;
> O'er hill and valley far and wide
> They waved in the warm wind; the sun
> Seemed shining upon every one,
> As though it loved it. . . . "
>
> [VI, 63]

The reign of Ragnar ("so great Ragnar's glory seemed / To Northern folk" [VI, 64]) is a renewal of the ancient glory of Sigurd and the Volsung line. Thus the renewing of the earth results from the irresistible impulsion of destiny.

As we have seen, "The Man Born to Be King" and "The Doom of King Acrisius" illustrate the emphasis on fate, though their primary import is not so much the impulsion of destiny on the hero as on those who would thwart it. "The Son of Croesus" is very like these tales in its treatment of prophecy and attempted avoidance, but here the prophesied act is the accidental death of an innocuous young prince, and there is little didactic meaning to be found in it, whereas in the other two tales the chastening of mortal hubris is emphasized. What "The Son of Croesus" accomplishes at this particular point (July) in *The Earthly Paradise* is the reiteration of the association of the Cain motif, intensified in this story, with the fate theme, although the futility of merely mortal striving is again an important point. Adrastus comes to Lydia as a result of having accidentally killed his brother in Phrygia, and, in extending hospitality to the stranger, Croesus unwittingly harbors the eventual slayer of his own son, Atys. Adrastus, driven to suicide by the guilt of his crime, is the type of the hapless victim of fate destroyed by the role he is destined to play: "The Gods are wearied for that still I live, / And with their will, why should I longer strive?" (IV, 158).

The crime of Adrastus is analogous to the early history of Bellerophon in "Bellerophon at Argos." He, like Adrastus, has unwittingly killed his brother and seeks asylum in Argos. But Bellerophon is to expiate his crime with great deeds and, in Lycia, will become the savior of the people by slaying the Chimera. More than any other hero in *The Earthly Paradise*, Bellerophon is envisaged as a godlike figure and is identified with the sun as life principle. He appears to Philonoë by a "high tower great and round" (VI, 198), surrounded by lilies and woodbine. The "green clad" Bellerophon suggests a fertility figure associated with this phallic tower. This passage makes explicit the role of the hero as a means of revitalization and renewal on a symbolic sexual level, associated with the sun: "he seemed to be / A piece of sunlight fallen down suddenly" (VI, 198). (The association of the king or hero with the sun is, of course, traditional, and Morris is quite fond of the analogy, as we shall see in the discussions of "The Lovers of Gudrun" and *Sigurd the Volsung*, which follow.)[9] Additionally, the tower, "wrought by long-dead men of ancient lore," is a relic of a heroic past age with which Bellerophon's deeds are associated. King Proetus' advice had earlier identified deeds of heroic valor with the past golden age:

> "O fair Bellerophon, like me, be wise,
> And set things good to win before thine eyes,
> Lands, and renown, and riches, and a life
> That knows from day to day so much of strife
> As makes men happy, since the age of gold
> Is past, if e'er it was, as a tale told."
>
> [VI, 80]

The adventure of the hero is a means of reconstituting the golden age both on a literal level by saving the people from some threat, usually in the form of a dragon or other monster, and on a symbolic vicarious level by substantiating through great deeds the lost values of the past. Thus Bellerophon, as hero, is the means of society's rebirth and renewal.

Although our concern is not with source material, Morris's omissions from the Bellerophon legend are interesting in light of our objective in this discussion of *The Earthly Paradise*, which is to establish a basis for understanding its unity of theme and viewpoint. Aside from the slaying of the Chimera, Bellerophon's best-known association is with Pegasus, the magical winged horse on which, after other adventures, he attempts to scale Mount Olympus. This was Milton's instinctive association with the legend (as in Bellerophon's blinding he found further grist for his mill), and it is an endeavor doomed to end in disaster, since it is an unexampled piece of hubris that can never succeed in Greek legend. But we have seen that such overtly Faustian acts also cannot succeed in the world of *The Earthly*

---

[9] See Campbell's remarks on the relationship of the monarch to the sun and his discussion of Odysseus as a solar hero, ibid., pp. 75, 162–77.

Paradise; such an attempt to place man on a level with the gods (that is, to attain immortality) is like the doomed voyage of the wanderers. The earthly paradise can be achieved only on a symbolic level, vicariously through the deeds of a hero or, as we shall see, through the sexual principle of physical generation. Morris, having endowed his Bellerophon with the most admirable heroic attributes, does not leave him as does the *Iliad* wandering alone, "eating his heart out, skulking aside from the trodden track of humanity."[10] Instead, he ends the tale with the accession of Bellerophon to the throne of Lycia, clad "in gold and royal gear, / Such as a King might bear in Saturn's reign" (VI, 274), looking forward to his marriage with Philonoë:

> And even as a man new made a God,
> When first he sets his foot upon the sod
> Of Paradise, and like a living flame
> Joy wraps him round, he felt, as now she came,
> Clear won at last, the thing of all the earth
> That made his fleeting life a little worth.
>
> [VI, 277]

Those protagonists of *The Earthly Paradise* who achieve the state of blessedness represented by some form of the earthly paradise, for example, Psyche, Ogier the Dane, or the hero of "The Land East of the Sun and West of the Moon," come to bliss through suffering and acquiescence, not through hubris.

A parallel omission occurs in Morris's treatment of the Alcestis story. What is to Browning the most significant feature of the legend—Alcestis' rescue from death by Hercules, which is the central episode of his "Balaustion's Adventure"—is entirely eliminated in Morris's "The Love of Alcestis," in which Alcestis remains irrecoverably dead, her life perpetuated only in the fame of her great sacrifice. A poignant expression of the need for resignation is sung by Apollo as he tends the herds of Admetus:

> O dwellers on the lovely earth,
> Why will ye break your rest and mirth
> To weary us with fruitless prayer;
> Why will ye toil and take such care
> For children's children yet unborn,
> And garner store of strife and scorn
> To gain a scarce-remembered name,
> Cumbered with lies and soiled with shame?
>
> [IV, 95]

---

[10] Richmond Lattimore, trans., *The Iliad of Homer* (Chicago, 1951), Book VI, ll. 201–2, p. 158.

While Euripides uses the Alcestis story as the basis for a problem play and Meredith sees Apollo's stay on earth as Admetus' herdsman as the subject of a paean to the sun-god's bringing of light to a rejoicing earth in "Phoebus with Admetus," the primary emphasis of Morris's story is the poignancy of the friendship between god and mortal. But it is implicitly a tale of fate and illustrates well the superiority of the Fates over the Olympians in the Greek view of life: Apollo, despite his love for Admetus, cannot effect a reversal of the Fates' decree of death. Although Apollo refers to the decrees of the gods (IV, 120), the passage in its entirety makes clear that the decrees are actually those of the Fates.

Throughout *The Early Paradise* Morris makes the point that earthly happiness is to be found only in acceptance of the cosmic plan, the existence of which, to his way of thinking, is indicated by his repeated inclusion of, and emphasis on, the fatalistic aspects of his sources. But such a view of life, if fatalistic, is not necessarily pessimistic; as we have indicated, such acceptance also makes possible the significant deeds of the great heroes. Bellerophon exhibits the acquiescence requisite to true heroism and at the same time accepts responsibility for whatever befalls. As he leaves Argos, his thoughts express his perception of the relationship between character and fate:

> "Now go I forth alone
> To do what in my life must needs be done,
> And in my own hands lies my fate, I think,
> And I shall mix the cup that I must drink:
> So be it. . . . "
>
> [VI, 122]

Thus the great hero Hercules is seen in "The Golden Apples" bending his will to the dictum of the Fates. Warned by one of the maidens of the curse laid on the golden fruit, Hercules stoically pursues his appointed task:

> "So be it," he said, "the Fates that drive me on
> Shall slay me or shall save; blessing or curse
> That followeth after when the thing is won
> Shall make my work no better now nor worse;
> And if it be that the world's heart must nurse
> Hatred against me, how then shall I choose
> To leave or take?—let your dread servant loose! "
>
> [VI, 12]

And so he faces the worm in the most suggestively emblematic scene of *The Earthly Paradise*. This adventure, plucked, as it were, from the continuum of Hercules' many labors, has a quality of stasis concentrated in this scene in the timeless garden that will remain when the world is "foredone" (VI, 12):

> Closer the coils drew, quicker all about
> The forked tongue darted, and yet stiff he stood. . . .
>
> . . . . .
>
> Bright in the sun he stood above the dead,
> Panting with fury; . . .
>
> . . . . .
>
> Silent and moveless ever stood the three;
> No change came o'er their faces, as his hand
> Was stretched aloft unto the sacred tree;
> Nor shrank they aught aback, though he did stand
> So close that tresses of their bright hair, fanned
> By the sweet garden breeze, lay light on him,
> And his gold fell brushed by them breast and limb.
>
> [VI, 13]

Hercules facing the serpent becomes the focal point of the tale itself, drawing attention to analogues occurring elsewhere in *The Earthly Paradise*. The Hesperides are one of the traditional locations of the Blessed Isles, or vestigial golden age, and the beautiful garden containing forbidden fruit laden with a curse and guarded by a serpent is suggestive of the garden of Genesis, scene of man's Fall from the paradisaical state. The combat between the hero and the serpent is, moreover, suggestive of the apocalyptic overcoming of the dragon foretold in the book of Revelation, the event which will bring in the millennium, that is, restore the golden age. This encounter elliptically symbolizes both the Fall and the redemption of mankind. This association is suggested in Tennyson's poem "The Hesperides":

> If the golden apple be taken
> The world will be overwise.
>
> . . . . .
>
> Father Hesper, Father Hesper, watch, watch, night and day,
> Lest the old wound of the world be healèd,
> The glory unsealèd,
> The golden apple stolen away,
> And the ancient secret revealèd.[11]

We have already noted how the hero's life is a paradigm of man's fall from grace, symbolized by the Cain motif, and man's salvation, accomplished through self-immolation in the predestined act of

---

[11] "Hesperides," ll. 63–72.

heroism that renews society. The hero-monster confrontation, then, is the quintessential act in the life of the culture hero, and Morris returns repeatedly to this motif.

As is well known, the dragon-slayer tale is one of the most prolific folktale types and is found figuring prominently in the heroic literature in which Morris delighted. Morris's dragon- or monster-slayers include not only Hercules, Perseus, and Bellerophon of *The Earthly Paradise* but Jason of *The Life and Death of Jason*, Sigurd of *Sigurd the Volsung*, and Beowulf of Morris's translation of the Old English epic. These dragons or monsters are not evil in the way that Spenser's, for example, are, for Morris is not concerned with the problems of the individual soul overcoming evil—his morality is not Christian. Morris's dragons are often as not harmlessly guarding their treasures when challenged by the heroes. Aside from the monsters slain by Beowulf, the only public threat occurring in *The Earthly Paradise* or the other poems is the Chimera killed by Bellerophon. Questions of good and evil are beside the point in these fated encounters, which are enactments of culminating processes set in motion by cosmic forces before the creation of the world, a fact glimpsed by Rolf when he dreamed of heroic death fighting either for or against Edward. There is much the same feeling of inevitability in these Morrisian heroic combats as in Hardy's "The Convergence of the Twain," the poem about the building of the *Titanic* while the "Immanent Will" fashions "a sinister mate" in the form of the iceberg.

The unalterable unfolding of destiny need not always be expressed in literal monster-slaying, of course. Morris's "The Lovers of Gudrun," based on the pseudohistorical *Laxdoela Saga*, is realistic in mode; yet the life of the Icelandic hero, Kiartan, follows the pattern of the legendary culture hero in a number of significant respects. Here the fated encounter is with the hero's own foster brother, Bodli, whose eventual slaying of Kiartan is foretold by the seer Guest. The close relationship of Kiartan and Bodli and their destined enmity recalls the Cain motif of other stories in *The Earthly Paradise* (Bodli, in fact, compares himself to Cain [V, 384]); in "The Lovers of Gudrun" the two men, like ship and iceberg, are symbolically united as "twin halves of one august event."[12] Their dialectical relationship is symbolically apprehended in terms of physical description. When Kiartan is first seen by Guest, he is "a tall youth whose golden head did gleam / In the low sun" (V, 267). Bodli, whose coloring is not described in the saga source, is "black-haired and tall" (V, 267) in Morris's tale.[13] Through-

---

[12] *Collected Poems of Thomas Hardy* (New York, 1925), p. 289.
[13] The opposition between fair and dark is stressed also in *Sigurd the Volsung*. A.

out, Morris associates Kiartan with the sun, not least significantly when, about to meet death in the ambush of Bodli and Gudrun's brothers, he offers a last challenge to Bodli: "Come, for the midday sun is over-bright, / And I am wearying for the restful night!" (V, 377). Kiartan's identification with the sun blends with his role as symbol of Iceland when the king of Norway, looking on the Icelanders, is blinded by the sun:

> his right [hand] did shade
> His eyes from the bright sun that 'gainst him blazed,
> As on the band of Icelanders he gazed.
>
> [V, 290]

The dead Kiartan is borne on his bier in a procession "As mournful as though dead with them they bore / The heart of Iceland" (V, 382). Kiartan is the dying sun of Iceland, a symbol of the crepuscular Viking civilization that succumbed, overripe, to the advancing Christian church, thenceforth to become even further removed from a heroic heritage.[14] Morris was moved by his visit to Laxdale to write: "Just think, though, what a mournful place this is—Iceland, I mean—setting aside the pleasure of one's animal life there, the fresh air, the riding and rough life, and feeling of adventure;—how every place and name marks the death of its short-lived eagerness and glory: . . . But Lord! what littleness and helplessness has taken the place of the old passion and violence that had place here once—and all is unforgotten; so that one has no power to pass it by unnoticed."[15]

"The Lovers of Gudrun" is itself like a paradigm of decay. When Guest visits the hall of Olaf Hauskuldson, he sees the "noble stories" of Norse mythology painted on the "high panelling and roof-boards," among them the "deeds of Thor":

> the fight in the far sea
> With him who rings the world's iniquity,
> The Midgard Worm; strife in the giants' land,
> With snares and mockeries thick on either hand,
> And dealings with the Evil One who brought
> Death even amid the Gods. . . .
>
> [V, 263–64]

This description, not found in *The Laxdoela Saga*, is a redaction of the Norse story of the Fall, the coming of strife into the world in the form

---

Margaret Arent points out correspondences in the saga sources. See her *Laxdoela Saga* (Seattle, 1964), p. 197, *n*. 4.

[14] This view of Icelandic history is not universally accepted, but it is advanced by Thorstein Veblen in his *Laxdaela Saga* (New York, 1925), pp. vi–xi.

[15] Quoted in Mackail, I, 259–60.

of the serpent, the Midgard Worm. The low-keyed realism of Morris's style in "The Lovers of Gudrun," perhaps the quality that has won it so much admiration among critics who are otherwise unimpressed with *The Earthly Paradise,* may be imitative of the tenor of these "latter days" when the mythic adventures of a more primitive society are no longer possible.[16] These paler deeds, the nature of which is, of course, dictated by the source, are appropriate to the facts of existence in an inferior and pallid age. The life of Kiartan exhibits the same paradigm in miniature. The strife that comes between the two houses of Herdholt and Bathstead because of Gudrun severs the "latter days" mourned by Olaf (V, 366) from the idyllic "past days, when fair and orderly / The world before our footsteps seemed to lie" (V, 354).

The spurious historicity of these events constituted one of the main attractions of the story for Morris.[17] His enthusiasm for the actuality of the scenes of the saga is shown in his letters written from Iceland:

> Olaf Peacock went about summer and winter after his live-stock, and saw to his hay-making and fishing, just as this little peak-nosed parson does; setting aside the coffee and brandy, his victuals under his hall "marked with famous stories" were just the same the little parson in his ten foot square parlour eats: I don't doubt the house stands on the old ground.
>
> I have seen many marvels and some terrible pieces of country; slept in the home-field of Njal's house, and Gunnar's, and at Herdholt: I have seen Bjarg, and Bathstead, and the place where Bolli was killed, and am now a half-hour's ride from where Gudrun died.[18]

The events of "The Lovers of Gudrun" considered as history substantiate in life the patterns to which Morris had already been attracted in folktale and heroic literature. But there are other significant aspects of these patterns, which we will consider next.

---

[16] See, for instance, Thompson, *Work of William Morris,* pp. 179–80.

[17] Arent, pp. xxiv–xxviii, discusses the curiously convincing style of the saga writers and the difficulties in separating truth from fiction in the Family Sagas.

[18] Quoted in Mackail, I, 260–61.

Chapter III

The Female Principle

WE HAVE CONSIDERED the hero's function as renewer of society, the act of heroism being the agency by which human society is restored to an approximation of the golden age, or primeval earthly paradise. An important related pattern in the characteristic heroic adventure is the visit of the hero to the otherworld, where he is usually aided by supernatural agencies, often a woman. The prominence of this pattern in Morris's work is not surprising inasmuch as he worked from traditional source material. This pattern is truly ubiquitous in mythology, heroic literature, romance, and folklore, to the extent that it has been termed *monomyth* by Joseph Campbell, who describes it thus: "A hero ventures forth from the world of common day into a region of supernatural wonder: fabulous forces are there encountered and a decisive victory is won: the hero comes back from this mysterious adventure with the power to bestow boons on his fellow man."[1] Further, folklorists and literary critics alike generally acknowledge the otherworld visited by the hero to be a metaphorical form of the earthly paradise, or primeval golden age, the concept of which, as we have noticed, is of paramount importance in Morris's work.[2] Indeed, Morris makes the connection explicit in "Ogier the Dane," as Morgan le Fay speaks to Ogier:

> "But I, who longed to share with thee my bliss,
> Am of the fays and live their changeless life,
> And like the Gods of old, I see the strife
> That moves the world, unmoved if so I will;
> For we the fruit that teaches good and ill
> Have never touched like you of Adam's race.
>
> . . . . .
>
> Know thou, that thou art come to Avallon,
> That is both thine and mine."
>
> [IV 230–31]

The association of Morgan le Fay with Avalon illustrates the tra-

[1] Campbell, *Hero*, p. 30.
[2] See, for instance, Howard Rollin Patch, *The Other World according to Descriptions in Medieval Literature* (Cambridge, Mass., 1950), pp. 1–5, and passim.

ditional combination of the otherworld and the supernatural woman, or fay.[3]

The usual forms of the otherworld are the underworld, the island, the garden (usually containing a fountain or one or more rivers), the hill or mountain, or the sky realm. There are many variations on these basic types; for instance, the otherworld may appear simply as a land across a river or other body of water, or a castle surrounded by a moat. The moated grange of Tennyson's "Mariana" derives much of its effective oppressiveness from its covert, otherworld associations, and the Lady of Shalott, leaving her island tower, is born into life (as well as borne unto death). The otherworld is usually recognizable by great beauty and fecundity evidenced in landscape and inhabitants, gorgeous fragrances, and—perhaps most frequently—its quality of timelessness, which is habitually conveyed in Morris's poems by the phenomenon of flower and fruit appearing together. The entrance to the underworld may be a hollow hill, cave, well, pit, hidden stairs, or even, as in Beowulf's visit to Grendel's lair, a pit underneath a body of water. Frequently a magical bridge or boat is the means of entering the otherworld across the water. Even Wordsworth's stolen boat in an autobiographical poem like *The Prelude* is an "elfin pinnace" in a more or less supernatural context, and the ferryman who conducts him home (after a significant nine months' absence) is "the Charon of the flood."[4] The mystical associations of sea voyages are not confined to literature: as Arthur was transported to Avalon, so were countless numbers of historical kings and heroes, as we know from archaeological excavations of funeral barges. Magical flight, sometimes on the backs of supernatural birds or other animals (some of Sinbad's adventures with eagles and rocs fit into this category), is also a means of transportation to the otherworld, although sometimes it may be reached more prosaically on foot or on horseback.[5]

The otherworld pattern is inherent in most of the tales of *The Earthly Paradise* (as it is in most of Morris's writings, owing to his predilection for traditional tales and themes), sometimes overtly, sometimes only by analogy to the characteristic patterns of the

[3] I am unaware of any definitive discussion of this point. An interesting discussion of Celtic traditions is contained in Tom Peete Cross's article "The Celtic Elements in the Lays of 'Lanval' and 'Graelant,' " *Modern Philology* 12 (1915), 585–644. The Celtic fay (or fée) is analogous to the Eves, Circes, Venuses, and other garden, island, or cavern temptresses of mythology and literature. See also Barbara Fass, *La Belle Dame sans Merci & the Aesthetics of Romanticism* (Detroit, 1974), especially chapter 1, "Seductress or Penitent: The Symbolic Otherworld."

[4] William Wordsworth, *The Prelude, or Growth of a Poet's Mind* (1850), I, 357–400, IV, 14.

[5] Patch's *Other World* contains a comprehensive discussion of otherworld characteristics.

folktale type being treated. On an overt level, there is the voyage of Hercules to the Hesperides, the voyage of Ogier the Dane on the magical boat, and Bharam's similar sea journey in "The Man Who Never Laughed Again." The faery palace in "The Watching of the Falcon" is a clear example, as is the otherworld found by Walter in "The Hill of Venus." Other tales contain obvious otherworld earmarks. For instance, Perseus' magical flight precedes his heroic adventures, as in "The Love of Alcestis" Admetus' journey to Iolchos to win his bride is undertaken in a magical chariot provided by Apollo and drawn by lion and boar yoked together. Admetus is instructed that on his return he must leave the chariot before crossing a certain stream and must not look back, recalling the story of Lot's wife leaving the cities of the plain, as well as Orpheus and Eurydice leaving the underworld. "The Lady of the Land" involves a visit to an underground apartment that has a number of characteristics of the otherworld:

> And in a strange place, lit as by a fire
> Unseen but near, he presently did stand;
> And by an odorous breeze his face was fanned,
> As though in some Arabian plain he stood,
> Anigh the border of a spice-tree wood.
>
> [IV, 130]

In this chamber, containing the wealth of a fallen civilization, "It seemed that time had passed on otherwhere" (IV, 130). On a more subliminal level is Bellerophon's voyage, after the false accusations of the queen Sthenoboea, to Lycia, the scene of his greatest deeds, where he is helped by a princess. (A similar pattern, including both the Potiphar's Wife motif and the journey to the otherworld inhabited by helpful women, is found in "The Lay of Sir Launfal" and "The Lay of Graelent" of Marie de France.) And in "The Man Born to Be King," Michael passes over both a stream and a moat to reach the castle inhabited by the princess who, after finding him sleeping by a fountain in the garden, marries him and saves his life.

Because the significant deed of heroism is usually performed in this metaphorical otherworld, or variety of earthly paradise, the hero's function is that of literally bringing together the real world, which he represents, with the otherworld, or earthly paradise, which he visits; and the effect of this mystical act is to cause the real world to conform to the conditions of the golden age symbolically represented by the otherworld. In this way the real world is saved or redeemed by the heroic act.

The continuing central importance of this mythic pattern in modern Western consciousness is attested by the manner in which it

repeatedly forms the basis for new works. Possibly the greatest of
twentieth-century novels, Thomas Mann's *Magic Mountain*, is, of
course, built upon the myth of the hero and his visit to the otherworld.
Hans Castorp's going to war at the end of the novel is an affirmation of
the ancient pattern: the hero (even when he is something of an
antihero) must at length find his destiny in action. In Morris's writings these symbolic manifestations of the earthly paradise are usually attained unwittingly by the hero in the course of answering some
compelling call to adventure or action. Bellerophon's legendary
storming of Olympus, as we have seen, was a doomed enterprise
because it was defiant and Promethean, qualities anathema to the
Greek idea of appropriate human conduct. Such a conscious and
hubristic effort to attain paradise, like the voyage of the wanderers,
cannot succeed in Morris's pagan cosmology. Thus Bellerophon's
ill-fated effort does not appear in the two Bellerophon tales of *The
Earthly Paradise*, and rightly so, because the Olympian attempt is not
consonant with the truly heroic fatalism with which Morris invests
his Bellerophon.

Morris does much the same thing again in "The Writing on the
Image"—he uses what fits his cosmology, ignores what does not. In
this tale the attainment of the otherworld, in the form of an underworld treasure chamber reached by hidden stairs, results in death for
the scholar who deciphers the writing on the image. The chill ending
with the greedy scholar trapped beneath the earth is Morris's own;
the medieval source, as Mackail and others have pointed out, ends
with his escape. In Morris's poetic scheme of things, a selfish lust for
riches and power cannot meet with success. The scholar, motivated
by the grossest of human passions, is even found contemplating the
creation of his own somewhat Oriental paradise:

> And if my soul I may not save
> In heaven, yet here in all men's eyes
> Will I make some sweet paradise,
> With marble cloisters, and with trees
> And bubbling wells and fantasies,
> And things all men deem strange and rare,
> And crowds of women kind and fair,
> That I may see, if so I please,
> Laid on the flowers, or mid the trees
> With half-clad bodies wandering.
> There, dwelling happier than the King,
> What lovely days may yet be mine!
> How shall I live with love and wine
> And music, till I come to die!

> [IV, 79]

Such motives stem neither from heroism nor from idealistic emotion. Significantly, the scene that meets the scholar's eye in the subterranean hall is reminiscent of the spectacle of death found by the wanderers on the mountaintop burial ground of the forest dwellers' kings:

> these were bodies dead and cold
> Attired in full royal guise,
> And wrought by art in such a wise
> That living they all seemed to be,
> Whose very eyes he well could see,
> That now beheld not foul or fair. . . .
>
> [IV, 81]

The scholar's attempt is not an act of heroism and can bring only annihilation, so complete that all traces of the image and the plate in the pavement are destroyed in a storm signaling the scholar's miserable end.

Those tales of *The Earthly Paradise* having more or less overt otherworld patterns tend toward failure; as a rule, only when the journey to the otherworld occurs on a subliminal level is the outcome sanguine. The basic folktale type of which these tales are variations is known as "The Man on a Quest for His Lost Wife."[6] In the simplest form of this worldwide folktale, the hero marries a supernatural woman and subsequently goes home on a visit, either forgetting his wife in favor of another woman or breaking some prohibition, thus losing his wife. He must then search for her, an undertaking usually requiring a visit to the otherworld, where they are reunited. Generally, in literary treatments of this pattern, the quest is unsuccessful. Keats's "La Belle Dame sans Merci" is perhaps the most famous work of literature based on this extraordinarily popular tale type and one which, as George Ford, among others, has demonstrated, worked powerfully on the Pre-Raphaelite sensibility.[7] The quiddity of Morris's morality is in no other wise so clearly revealed as in the fact that whereas Keats's knight is a victim of the cruel fay (if we take the most obvious and, perhaps, simplistic, reading of the poem),[8] Morris characteristically explains the failure of the hero by some fault in his character or motives.

Three tales of this pattern end with utter desolation. Bharam, the protagonist of "The Man Who Never Laughed Again," is forever

---

[6] Tale Type 400 in Thompson's *Types of the Folktale*, pp. 128 ff.

[7] See *Keats and the Victorians: A Study of His Influence and Rise to Fame, 1821–1895* (Hamden / London, 1962), especially p. 152. See also E. P. Thompson, *William Morris: Romantic to Revolutionary* (1955; rev. ed. New York, 1977), pp. 10–21.

[8] For a more complex and subtle reading see Earl R. Wasserman, *The Finer Tone: Keats' Major Poems* (Baltimore, 1953), pp. 65–83.

banished from the otherworld for giving in to the temptation to use
the golden key and drink from the cup that promised everlasting
fame. Having been tainted even momentarily by egoism, he can never
be redeemed, no matter how great his subsequent suffering. "The
Watching of the Falcon" is more complex. The king, wishing for the
love of the fay as his reward for the vigil, is admonished by her:

> "Better it were that men should live
> As beasts and take what earth can give,
> The air, the warm sun and the grass,
> Until unto the earth they pass,
> And gain perchance nought worse than rest,
> Than that not knowing what is best
> For sons of men, they needs must thirst
> For what shall make their lives accurst.
>
> "Therefore I bid thee now beware,
> Lest getting something seeming fair
> Thou com'st in vain to long for more,
> Or lest the thing thou wishest for
> Make thee unhappy till thou diest,
> Or lest with speedy death thou buyest
> A little hour of happiness
> Or lazy joy with sharp distress."
>
> [IV, 173]

The king makes the same mistake as the wanderers—because he
cannot forego what is forbidden to mortals, he is condemned to lose
all that is meaningful or comforting in human life: his children come
to ruin, his kingdom is overrun by barbarians, and he is murdered in
his sleep by traitors.

> Great among other kings, I said
> He was before he first was led
> Unto that castle of the fays;
> But soon he lost his happy days,
> And all his goodly life was done.
>
> [IV, 179]

One of the basic elements of "The Man on a Quest for His Lost Wife"
is the desertion or forgetting of the supernatural wife. Morris's early
poems "The Sailing of the Sword" and "Welland River" may be read
in this context, and several tales of *The Earthly Paradise* not only
include this motif but center on it. "The Death of Paris" is the clearest
example. In this tale Paris returns to the sacred groves of Ida, where
he had once been happy with the nymph Oenone. He has not only
forgotten her in his passion for Helen, but desires to be healed so that

he may return to Helen's arms. Unlike Tennyson in his two poems on the subject, Morris concentrates not on the despair of Oenone but on Paris's self-induced alienation from the paradisaical world represented by the groves of Ida. It is the perfidy of Paris that bars him from the salvation of the fay-nymph, who here represents the lost innocence of a golden past:

> The image of his youth and faith gone by
> She seemed to be, for one short minute born
> To make his shamed lost life seem more forlorn.
>
> [V,17]

"The Lovers of Gudrun," though realistic in mode, contains the skeleton of the same tale type. Kiartan's desertion of Gudrun (rationalized, to be sure, as a patriotic excursion), his attraction to Ingibiorg in Norway, his return to Iceland and his discovery that Gudrun is lost to him, and his subsequent marriage (which repeats the forgetting motif) fit the pattern of the quest for the lost wife. Kiartan's desertion and Gudrun's consequent revenge constitute a major pattern in the story, to which the pattern of the enmity between brothers ending in treachery and death has been assimilated by the saga author. Kiartan's tragedy directly results from his "betrayal" of Gudrun, even though it is a somewhat unwitting betrayal.

Several analogous tales of *The Earthly Paradise* do end with the protagonist's attainment of the otherworld, or paradisaical state, on an overt level, but there are important differences. One of these is "Ogier the Dane." Ogier is destined from birth to be transported to the "happy country" (IV, 214) of Avalon by Morgan le Fay, the sixth of the fays who visit his cradle. Rescued from imminent death in the magic boat, he is transported, willy-nilly, to the otherworld, the reality of which he had not suspected, much less striven to prove. Ogier, in his awareness of his fallen state, considers himself unworthy to enter the "garden fit for utmost bliss":

> He said: "O God, a sinner I have been,
> And good it is that I these things have seen
> Before I meet what Thou hast set apart
> To cleanse the earthly folly from my heart;
> But who within this garden now can dwell,
> Wherein guilt first upon the world befell?"
>
> [IV, 225]

Only at the suggestion of the fay does he return to earth as a savior-warrior. Passively accepting his role, he has completely forgotten his fairy mistress and is about to marry the queen of France when summoned back to Avalon by Morgan le Fay. He does her bidding as though hypnotized: "and in all he seemed / To do these things e'en as a man who dreamed" (IV, 252). The key to Ogier's unqualified reception into the earthly paradise is his heroic passivity and freedom from hubris. One of Morris's most acquiescent and humble heroes, he submits to the edicts of fate almost unconsciously.

"The Land East of the Sun" is a straightforward variation of the search for the supernatural wife. The swan maiden is an obvious and well-known form of the supernatural woman, and the otherworld to which she is native is likewise overtly presented. John's quest, though undertaken quite consciously, is motivated by the most idealistic of loves (he blithely ignores the adulterous advances of his brother's wife, Thorgerd, and thus avoids the pitfall of falsity to his fairy wife). Though his quest is successful, the ending is not unalloyed. Morris vitiates it in two ways—first by the double distancing in narration, then by projecting an end to John's happiness. The tale of John's search for his swan-maiden wife is told by a character in the dream of Gregory the Star-gazer, who is a character in a tale told by one of the wanderers. When it is recalled that the wanderers themselves are characters within the idle singer's story, the number of removes from reality has the effect of cumulative distancing, which makes the otherworld associated more than ever with dreaming and fantasy rather than actuality. The story is described several times as an "idle dream" (V, 118, 120). As if this were not sufficient to dampen the spirits of seekers after paradise, it is made clear within the story of John and his supernatural bride that their happiness is not for eternity:

> No more this side of death to part—
> —No more, no more—Full soft I say
> Their greetings were that happy day,
> As though in pensive semblance clad;
> For fear their faces over-glad
> This certain thing should seem to hide,
> That love can ne'er be satisfied.
>
> [V, 118]

A much more sanguine outlook emerges in Morris's version of a related tale-type variant, "The Story of Cupid and Psyche," the outcome of which is singular within the context of *The Earthly Paradise*.[9] While resurrection from the dead does not occur in *The Earthly Paradise* (witness Morris's omission in "The Love of Alcestis" of Alcestis' return from death; similarly, Ogier the Dane, like Arthur, is

---

[9] The Cupid and Psyche story is a variant of a tale type related to Type 400, classified by Stith Thompson as Type 425, "The Search for the Lost Husband." See *Types of the Folktale*, pp. 140–42.

carried to Avalon before he dies), Psyche, at the end of her ordeal, attains immortality without going through death—she is in fact translated. Her "new birth" (IV, 73) is attained through arduous suffering and self-immolation and she, like John of "The Land East of the Sun," is motivated throughout not by pride or selfishness but by love. She is literally chastened by Love (in the person of Venus) so that she might be united with Love (Cupid). The literal love union between a mortal and the deity of love is repeated in "The Hill of Venus." This redaction of the Tannhäuser legend is, interestingly enough, the last of the tales of *The Earthly Paradise* and makes explicit the connection between the numerous tales that are variants of the search for the supernatural wife and the prominent treatment given to Venus all through the work. Here Venus is the supernatural wife, the fay associated with the otherworld.[10] As the song to Venus makes clear, she is "Born to give peace to souls that strive" (VI, 290). Because death lies ever at the end of every road, however glorious, mortals need the solace of her gifts. And Venus has "no cloud to raise her from the earth" (VI, 294); she embodies the earthly enjoyment of physical love. This is the "earthly paradise." A place where "two sundered lovers" might meet is "as the one dream of heaven" (VI, 293). The attainment of perfect love is equated with immortality:

> Then a great longing would there stir in him,
> That all those kisses might not satisfy;
> Dreams never dreamed before would gather dim
> About his eyes, and trembling would he cry
> To tell him how it was he should not die;
> To tell him how it was that he alone
> Should have a love all perfect and his own.
>
> [VI, 297]

Appropriately, it is Artemis, or Diana, the principle of asceticism and celibacy, in her manifestation as the moon, who arouses in the knight of Morris's tale an awareness of his baseness according to the standards of the mortal world he has left:

> From out a gleaming cloud the moon did break;
> Till, mid her balmy sleep, toward him she turned,
> And into his soul her touch his baseness burned.
>
> [VI, 300]

But Venus is at last victorious; Walter returns to the cavern in

> the ancient wood,
> Wild with sour waste and rough untended tree,

[10] This aspect of the legend was noticed by Baring-Gould, pp. 209–29.

> Which, long before the coming of the Rood,
> Men held a holy place in Germany.
>
> [VI, 281]

The result of Walter's return is not told; it must be inferred from the blossoming of the Pope's staff in a symbolic breaking through of eternity into the mortal world of time:

> With a great cry he sprang up; in his hand
> He held against the sky a wondrous thing,
> That might have been the bright archangel's wand,
> Who brought to Mary that fair summoning;
> For lo, in God's unfaltering timeless spring,
> Summer, and autumn, had that dry rod been,
> And from its barrenness the leaves sprang green,
>
> And on its barrenness grew wondrous flowers,
> That earth knew not; and on its barrenness
> Hung the ripe fruit of heaven's unmeasured hours;
> And with strange scent the soft dusk did it bless,
> And glowed with fair light as earth's light grew less.
>
> [VI, 325]

This token of renewal and rebirth, recalling the trees hanging with blossoms and fruit found in the otherworld by John in "The Land East of the Sun" and by the king of "The Watching of the Falcon," is symbolic of the regenerative effect of physical love triumphant over ascetic systems. The sexuality Morris celebrates has a wholesome, innocent quality about it; it is a naive physicality wholly lacking awareness of sin; thus Morris's poem is quite different from Swinburne's treatment of the legend, "Laus Veneris," which drips with the consciousness of sinful sensuality secretly and guiltily to be indulged in defiance of God until the final trump shall sound. Morris, in short, is much more the pagan than is Swinburne. In "The Hill of Venus" the here and now of paganism triumphs over the hereafter of Christianity. But Christianity is only one form of asceticism; what it stands for in Morris's world view is represented in the classical stories by the worship of Diana.

The opposition of Venus and Diana is introduced with the first tale of *The Earthly Paradise*, "Atalanta's Race." As the Argument states, the story tells how "Milanion, . . . outrunning Atalanta with the help of Venus, gained the virgin and wedded her" (III, 85). When Milanion first comes upon the town of King Schoeneus, he finds a scene of bucolic fertility, described in terms appropriate for the beauties of the otherworld:

The folk were busy on the teeming land,
And man and maid from the brown furrows cried,
Or midst the newly-blossomed vines did stand,
And as the rustic weapon pressed the hand
Thought of the nodding of the well-filled ear,
Or how the knife the heavy bunch should shear.

Merry it was: about him sung the birds,
The spring flowers bloomed along the firm dry road,
The sleek-skinned mothers of the sharp-horned herds
Now for the barefoot milking-maidens lowed.

[III, 86]

This garden vision is succeeded by a spectacle of death, death which results directly from repudiation of the life-principle of generation metaphorically implied in the description of natural fruitfulness. A race is being held between Atalanta, "like Diana clad" (III, 87), who has sworn virginity, and the latest of a number of luckless suitors, who is summarily put to the sword immediately following his defeat. King Schoeneus presides over the affair, and beneath his throne is a "golden image of the sun, / A silver image of the Fleet-foot one" (III, 87), images that reiterate the opposition of the benign and fructifying influence of Apollo, the sun, with his cold and wrathful twin sister Diana, the moon.

This juxtaposition of beauty and fertility with death recalls the pattern set up in the Prologue, in which the wanderers, eschewing the here and now in their search for life eternal, are repeatedly confronted with death. In "Atalanta's Race," however, death is directly related to the principle of celibacy, itself implicitly a denial of the validity of the here and now, practiced by Atalanta as a devotee of Diana. In Atalanta the life of the spirit predominates: "She seemed all earthly matters to forget," at the beginning of the race, and "some divine thought softened all her face" upon winning (III, 87–88).

Milanion's prayer to Venus makes explicit the relationship between sexual love and the lost golden age:

"O set us down together in some place
Where not a voice can break our heaven of bliss,
Where nought but rocks and I can see her face,
Softening beneath the marvel of thy grace,
Where not a foot our vanished steps can track—
The golden age, the golden age come back!"

[III, 97]

Venus' reply indicates that when Atalanta "Diana's raiment must unbind," the world will seem "blessed with Saturn's clime" (III, 100).

The golden age being forever gone, man can recapture its bliss only in moments of physical passion. Venus signals her granting of his prayer by appearing to Milanion in a vision of light attended by delicious fragrances, an epiphany echoed in several subsequent tales.

In "Atalanta's Race" the Judeo-Christian theme of man's temptation and Fall, represented metaphorically by his discovery of carnality, is, characteristically for Morris, reversed. Atalanta succumbs to the temptation of the golden apples, but her Fall is the means of her salvation, as Venus indicates to Milanion. He may "live to save / The cruel maiden from a loveless grave" (III, 99). Atalanta is indeed "Made happy that the foe the prize hath won, / She weeps glad tears for all her glory done" (III, 104). The story ends with a celebration of Venus and marriage. Thus, in this tale, as throughout *The Earthly Paradise*, Venus is triumphant. In this respect Morris follows the pattern of medieval treatments of the garden presided over by Venus Genetrix, "the renewer of life."[11]

All the tales do not end so happily as "Atalanta's Race," nor are all of them concerned with wooing and wedding. But the Venus-Diana opposition recurs in the manner of a leitmotiv as the monthly feasts continue through the year. In "The Doom of King Acrisius" Venus is the benefactress of the imprisoned Danaë, who, in her misery, prays to Diana for freedom and then for death (III, 176–77). Diana does not hear, but Venus does and intercedes with Jove to circumvent the efforts of Acrisius to prevent Danaë's giving birth:

> "great dishonour is it unto me
> That such a maiden lives so wretchedly;
> And great dishonour is it to us all
> That ill upon a guiltless head should fall
> To save a King from what we have decreed."
>
> [III, 179]

Thus Morris, linking two great themes of *The Earthly Paradise*, makes Venus the agent of destiny. She is appropriately associated with springtime and rebirth, which must recur as the seasons change through their preappointed cycles:

> Now therewithal went Venus to the sea
> Glad of her father's words, and, as she went,
> Unseen the gladness of the spring she sent
> Across the happy lands o'er which she moved,
> Until all men felt joyous and beloved.
>
> [III, 179]

---

[11] See Lovejoy and Boas, who point out that the praise of Venus is accompanied by a

The theme of Venus triumphant and beneficent occurs centrally in "Pygmalion and the Image" and "The Story of Acontius and Cydippe." In both, Venus answers the prayers of a lover and is associated with the beloved. In the former tale the statue brought to life by the goddess wears the saffron garment of Venus in token of her visitation when, in giving of the gown, she recalls the love of Psyche for Cupid: "Now herewith shalt thou love no less / Than Psyche loved my son in days of old" (IV, 207). The love of Pygmalion and Galatea transforms the earth into a paradise, as Pygmalion says: "thy blessed birth / Has made a heaven of this once lonely earth" (IV, 205). Galatea's transformation from stone to flesh is a literal example of the power of Venus, Love, as bringer of life. Galatea's birth is analogous to the "new birth" of Psyche, also effected by the power of Love.

In "The Story of Acontius and Cydippe" Venus appears to Acontius hand in hand with Cydippe in a vision. Her appearance is accompanied by symbolic tokens of victory over time and the seasons, recalling other Morrisian descriptions of the otherworld:

> Round Venus' feet
> Outbroke the changing spring-flowers sweet
> From the parched earth of autumn-tide.
>
> [V, 147]

Here, as elsewhere in *The Earthly Paradise*, Diana is the "dreadful Queen" (V, 133) who rules her maiden subjects with fear. It is she who visits the ghastly punishment on the lady of "The Lady of the Land" for the violation of her vows (IV, 136–37), she who must be appeased in order to banish the serpents from the bridal chamber of Admetus and Alcestis. By contrast, Venus at her most ill-tempered is more mischievous than malicious—although cruel to Psyche, she repents her torment of her in the end. Even in "The Ring Given to Venus," where she appears as one of a hellish company led by Satan (in a treatment of the traditional idea that pagan deities became demons upon the advent of Christianity), she is guilty only of accepting the ring given to her image in a moment of unfortunate disregard of her latent powers. In "The Death of Paris," where she might be blamed as the cause of the general Trojan debacle, the judgment of Paris is not mentioned.

Venus, then, is a major force in the tales of *The Earthly Paradise*, and her appearance usually signals an identification of paradisaical bliss with sexual love. Far from being merely a recurrent theme linking some of the tales, this reiterated association is the basis of the unity of

---

"consequent denunciation of celibacy as inimical to life and contrary to Nature's plan for the maintenance of the world" (p. 281).

the entire work—the individual tales, the interior framework of the
wanderers' story, and the overall frame of the idle singer's story
contained in the month poems.

It is fairly clear that the idle singer is the narrator of the month
poems which divide the pairs of verse tales told by the wanderers.
Most writers on Morris assume also, following Mackail, that the
month poems, telling in somewhat vague terms of a gradual
estrangement between the narrator and his beloved, are autobiographical. In Mackail's timid words, the autobiography is "so delicate and so outspoken that it must needs be left to speak for itself."[12]
Now that time has made discretion unnecessary, we may state baldly
that the month poems express Morris's feelings during the period of
Jane Morris's affair, or emotional involvement, with Rossetti. Although we cannot know for certain, it seems probable that the Morrises' estrangement was not so much caused by Rossetti as that the
Rossetti affair resulted from the Morrises' estrangement, which, in
turn, had as its primary cause a fundamental incompatibility of
temperament as well as background. But this does not mean that
Morris was capable of accepting the fact of his former mentor's
passion for his wife with equanimity; the available facts indicate
unmistakably that he was not. Morris's dedication of *The Earthly
Paradise* to his wife takes on a certain wistful pathos in light of what
we now know about this triangular relationship, but the point is that
the meaning of *The Earthly Paradise* is ultimately realized through the
medium of personal experience and emotion.

The progression of sentiment through the series of twelve poems is
from hope to wanhope, as man's life is repeatedly shown to be
anomalous within the world of nature. The seasons pass in their
appointed rounds, love fails to renew itself, the singer's yearning for
the happiness of the past is unsatisfied. He welcomes March with
hope for life, even though the burden of his death-awareness makes
him unable to greet the new year with the unqualified joy of birds
"Unmindful of the past or coming days." (Morris's spring song is
halfway between Chaucer's General Prologue and Eliot's "The Waste
Land" in attitude.) Time and death isolate the singer from the rebirth
of unconscious nature, but, paradoxically, it is the ever-closeness of
death that enhances all human joy:

> Ah, what begetteth all this storm of bliss
> But Death himself, who crying solemnly,
> E'en from the heart of sweet Forgetfulness,
> Bids us "Rejoice, lest pleasureless ye die.

12 Mackail, I, 210.

Within a little time must ye go by.
Stretch forth your open hands, and while ye live
Take all the gifts that Death and Life may give."

[III, 82][13]

The apostrophe to April reiterates the hope of springtime and rebirth: "The hopes and chances of the growing year, / Winter forgotten long, and summer near" (III, 169). Yet the death of winter ever hovers, even in summer, recalling that March was greeted as "Slayer of the winter":

When Summer brings the lily and the rose,
She brings us fear; her very death she brings
Hid in her anxious heart, the forge of woes.

[III, 169][14]

The singer's hope is even now mingled with despair, a longing "for that which never draweth nigh."

"May," addressed directly to the singer's beloved, tells of a dream of love ending with the light dawning upon a "sight of Eld and Death" (echoing the experiences of the wanderers in the Prologue). The music of Love had momentarily vanquished death; "The world had quite forgotten it must die" (IV, 1). "June" expresses the mood of a morning not yet vexed by "thought of storm" and begs that waking will not end the "rare happy dream" with "hopes and fears" left behind (IV, 87). This fleeting happiness is found in a rural garden spot, which anticipates the not-yet-discovered Kelmscott:

By this sweet stream that knows not of the sea,
That guesses not the city's misery,
This little stream whose hamlets scarce have names,
This far-off, lonely mother of the Thames.

[IV, 87]

This setting seems "far-off" not only in space but in time, in a golden age when the stream has not yet engendered the hideous Thames of the Prologue. Momentarily the singer has realized felicity but is yet aware enough of reality to know that the morning will be vexed, and the hopes and fears yet exist, though left behind. He is, in other words, conscious that his short joy is a dream, however he may try to believe in his temporary miniature paradise.

"July" reiterates the alienation of man from the rebirth of inani-

---

[13] Cf. the song of Orpheus from *Jason*, "O death, that maketh life so sweet" (*Works*, II, 176).
[14] Cf. "The Story of Acontius and Cydippe" (*Works*, V, 147), where Venus is associated with the lily and rose.

mate nature, repeating the carpe diem theme of "March" in a more desperate key (and suggesting the mood of Fitzgerald's *Rubáiyát*):

> Ah love! although the morn shall come again,
> And on new rose-buds the new sun shall smile,
> Can we regain what we have lost meanwhile?
>
> [IV, 143]

The singer is unable to recapture the happiness of the golden past—the earthly paradise is lost forever.

> E'en now the west grows clear of storm and threat,
> But midst the lightning did the fair sun die—
> Ah, he shall rise again for ages yet,
> He cannot waste his life; but thou and I?
>
> [IV, 143]

The laments for waste and loss are repeated in "August," and this time the shortness of mortal life is contrasted with the eons of time the English countryside has seen pass:

> Across the gap made by our English hinds,
> Amidst the Roman's handiwork, behold
> Far off the long-roofed church; the shepherd binds
> The withy round the hurdles of his fold
> Down in the foss the river fed of old,
> That through long lapse of time has grown to be
> The little grassy valley that you see.
>
> [IV, 187]

"September," perhaps the most poignant of all the month poems, expresses complete resignation to the loss of past happiness:

> Look long, O longing eyes, and look in vain!
> Strain idly, aching heart, and yet be wise,
> And hope no more for things to come again
> That thou beheldest once with careless eyes!
> Like a new-wakened man thou art, who tries
> To dream again the dream that made him glad
> When in his arms his loving love he had.
>
> [V, 1]

The autumn, despite the fruition it bears of "springtide's hope / Looked for through blossoms," can now take no joy in beginnings, which in retrospect have taken on the semblance of dreams, but would fain shade "its sad eyes from the rising sun / And weeps at eve because the day is done" (V, 1). This despite the singer's earlier vision in "April" of the fresh life of midspring clinging "About the fainting

autumn's sweet decay / When in the earth the hopeful seed they lay"
(III, 169).

"October," addressed to the beloved, evokes a scene of the dying
year dominated by relics of the dead past, contrasted with the "unchanging sea," here a symbol of eternity:

> O Love, turn from the unchanging sea, and gaze
> Down these grey slopes upon the year grown old,
> A-dying mid the autumn-scented haze,
> That hangeth o'er the hollow in the wold,
> Where the wind-bitten ancient elms enfold
> Grey church, long barn, orchard, and red-roofed stead,
> Wrought in dead days for men a long while dead.
>
> [V, 122]

The singer, long since wakened from dreams of love and eternity by
dawnings of Eld and Death, is attempting to make his beloved see too
that mortals must not identify themselves with the unchanging, but
must realize the shortness of their existence. He is then tempted by
the thought of dying with the year, of losing himself in a capitulation
to the rhythms of nature. But the year has fulfilled itself, it is "Too
satiate of life to strive with death," whereas he has not had "enough of
life and love" (V, 122). Thus once more the singer is unable to assimilate himself to the great life cycle of the earth.

"November" presents the bleakest vision yet of man's insignificance in the cycle of ages, in which only change itself is changeless:

> Yea, I have looked and seen November there;
> The changeless seal of change it seemed to be,
> Fair death of things that, living once, were fair;
> Bright sign of loneliness too great for me,
> Strange image of the dread eternity,
> In whose void patience how can these have part,
> These outstretched feverish hands, this restless heart?
>
> [V, 206]

"December" continues the theme of man's insignificance, now conceived spatially in a vision of the immensity of the skies:

> Pale stars, bright moon, swift cloud make heaven so vast
> That earth left silent by the wind of night
> Seems shrunken 'neath the grey unmeasured height.
>
> [VI, 1]

The insignificance of the earth itself amid the infinity of the cosmos
makes the memory of human love more than ever like a dream.

In "January," the singer's dying hope is cruelly revived by a glance, and the indifference of the heavens of "December" is echoed paradoxically in the ecstatic description of the beloved's eyes:

> O eyes of heaven, as clear thy sweet soul blazed
> On mine a moment! O come back again,
> Strange rest and dear amid the long dull pain?
>
> [VI, 65]

But "February" reveals that, of all things mortal, only hope and pain endure, like the "unseen corn" and "leafless elms" that await the spring:

> Shalt thou not wonder that it liveth yet,
> The useless hope, the useless craving pain,
> That made thy face, that lonely noontide, wet
> With more than beating of the chilly rain?
> Shalt thou not hope for joy new born again,
> Since no grief ever born can ever die
> Through changeless change of seasons passing by?
>
> [VI, 175]

The "changeless change of seasons" has now been apprehended in terms of the major spheres of human knowledge and experience: botanically, in the cycles of flowers and trees; geologically, in the shifting formations of rivers and valleys; archaeologically, in the remnants of rising and waning civilizations—the Roman roads and the barns and steads of past centuries; astronomically, in the smallness of the earth itself in the vast movements of the heavens. All these things preach resignation to the inevitable, yet the singer cannot extinguish his yearning for love, which would break through the cycle and renew the golden past. But joy cannot be newborn again; his earthly paradise is forever lost.

The quest of the singer to be reunited with his beloved is very like the quest for the supernatural wife in so many of the tales of *The Earthly Paradise*, a quest explored in many transmutations of circumstance, recurring like a leitmotiv in an opera. His journey to the otherworld, or paradise, with which his beloved is associated is realized symbolically in the progress of the poems through the seasons, but his consciousness of loss and waste is the only harvest of the paradisaical spring and summer. Like the wanderers, the idle singer fails to attain his goal. Like them, he must accept Eld and Death—he must resign himself to the human condition.

Part Two
The Epic Impulse

Introduction to Part Two

THE ZEITGEIST of the nineteenth century, which prompted such gigantic prose undertakings as Balzac's *La Comèdie Humaine* and the Barsetshire and Palliser novels of Trollope, had its effect on the poets as well. Hardy responded to the impulse in both genres: his Wessex novels, placed in chronological order according to setting, span almost the entire century from the Napoleonic wars (*The Trumpet–Major*) to 1889 (*Tess*); and he was in later years to depict in detail his conception of the entire cosmic order underlying the human events of the Napoleonic wars in his huge poetic drama, *The Dynasts*. There is evidence that *The Brothers Karamazov* is in fact only half of the work planned by Dostoevski, and Wordsworth's *Prelude* was conceived as an introduction to a massive poem to be called *The Recluse, or Views on Man, Nature, and Society*. Browning's *Ring and the Book* is, in one sense, a re-creation of the decadent society of the late Italian Renaissance, and Wagner's operatic tetralogy, *Der Ring des Nibelungen*, which required twenty-five years from conception to completion, results from the same impulse: meant to redeem modern Germany, it is a re-creation of the mythic beginnings of the German people. The development over a period of nearly thirty years of *Idylls of the King* from the first four narratives of 1859 into its final twelve-book form shows that the illustrious poet laureate of England felt too the spirit of nineteenth-century gigantism. These enormous works were anything but vagaries on the part of their authors—they were well received by the public, who were fully able to appreciate their immense scope. The mammoth, forty-thousand-line *Festus* of Spasmodic poet Philip James Bailey was extraordinarily popular in Victorian England. William Morris, author of *The Earthly Paradise*, *The Life and Death of Jason*, and *The Story of Sigurd the Volsung and the Fall of the Niblungs*, was a man of his time.

The Jason and Bellerophon stories, both of which Morris planned as part of *The Earthly Paradise*, seem to have taken on lives of their own as they were being written. *Jason* grew to epic proportions and could not be confined within the limits of its parent work, while the Bellerophon story constitutes two segments of *The Earthly Paradise*, the only legend so treated by Morris. This fecundity bore additional fruit in the form of *Sigurd the Volsung*, which is twice as long as the

Volsunga Saga, on which it is based. Morris's ability to amplify a tale, condemned by some modern critics as mere boring verbosity or, at best, monotony in the medieval manner, is, rather, a manifestation of an instinctive attraction to the epic form that is not only a response to the spirit of the age but a fulfillment of tradition. For the pastoral, to which *The Earthly Paradise* conforms in several ways, was in the Renaissance considered the proper province of the epic poet's first attempt. Virgil's *Eclogues* and Spenser's *The Shepherd's Calendar* are the best-known examples. The seasonal framework and the reiterated golden age theme are elements that are obviously pastoral, but the similarities do not end with these. Robert Kellogg and Oliver Steele, who discuss the pastoral in the context of the Renaissance tradition, say this about the pastoral as a vehicle for social comment:

> Common to both the biblical and the classical pastoral traditions as they were inherited by the Renaissance was a sometimes harsh satire. The figure of Piers the Plowman, for example, became a symbol of social and religious revolution in the fifteenth and sixteenth centuries. Life in both the courts of princes and the higher reaches of the ecclesiastical hierarchy was often held up in bitterly critical contrast to the millennial ideal of pastoral existence. This pastoral ideal was a kind of synthesis of Christian apocalypse, Stoic ethical values, and the classical myth of the Golden Age. It represented, in the simplest Christian terms, the social perfection that would be achieved only with the captivity and destruction of Satan and his worldly agents—a resurrected Garden of Eden.[1]

Though Morris is not concerned with the Christian problems of Satan and sin, *The Earthly Paradise* is yet a work related to a major literary tradition—one that perhaps may be called "pastoral social comment." Morris's later prose work about a medieval peasants' revolt, *A Dream of John Ball*, is another manifestation of this same interest, clearly recalling *Piers Plowman*, and the Utopian *News from Nowhere* is similarly related to this tradition. Further, the self-effacing narrators of these naively written later works are very like the idle singer of *The Earthly Paradise*, and all are quite like the humble shepherd-poet of Spenser as well as Chaucer's modest narrator.[2]

Similarly, *Jason* and *Sigurd* follow in somewhat loose form the traditions of the epic, both being long narrative poems concerned in the main with the life and exploits of a single great hero, although *Sigurd* follows the saga source in beginning with the history of the

---

[1] Introduction, *The Faerie Queene, I and II, The Mutability Cantos, and Selections from the Minor Poetry of Edmund Spenser* (New York: Odyssey Press, 1965), p. 439.

[2] Since this paragraph was first written, a comprehensive study of this subject has been published. See Blue Calhoun, *The Pastoral Vision of William Morris: The Earthly Paradise* (Athens, Ga., 1975).

Volsungs. But the finer technical points of genre distinctions are not our concern, nor is it our purpose to point out Morris's "sentimentalizing" deviations from his source material.[3] Both poems are indisputably very different from their ancient antecedents, and rightly so, as Victorian England was quite different from Homeric Greece and thirteenth-century Iceland. Whatever critics may think, Morris himself thought he was writing epics, or heroic poetry, and it behooves us to consider his reasons for thinking so. It is interesting that the subject matter of Morris's two epics should have inspired operas as well. (I refer, of course, to Wagner's *Ring* cycle and Cherubini's *Médée*, in which Tietjens's tour-de-force performances at Drury Lane between 1865 and 1870 doubtless did much to call the attention of the public to the story of Jason and Medea. Possibly this accounts for some of the success of Morris's poem.) The opera—aristocratic, highly stylized, and heroic in scale—is an art form analogous in many ways to the epic.

The traditional function of heroic poetry in the society for which it is composed is educative. Though, strictly speaking, the "highest cultural role" of the oral epics may have been "the education of princes," they formed as well an important societal function, for the lesson the princes were to learn, as we are told by Robert Scholes and Robert L. Kellogg in *The Nature of Narrative*, was that "the preservation of an ordered society is the highest good and the goal toward which the hero's physical and intellectual discipline is bent." Werner Jaeger in his *Paideia: The Ideals of Greek Culture* sees the aim of heroic poetry as "the creation and perpetuation of a heroic ideal." Its "objective picture of life as a whole" makes its "educational aim and influence . . . far greater than that of all other types of poetry." The double level of action in the Homeric epics shows the relationship between "human purpose and action" and the "higher purpose of the ruling gods." Jaeger describes the effect of Homer's poetry in terms that could equally apply to *Jason* and *Sigurd*. The fact, he says, that Homer "holds the gods to be implicated in every human action and suffering obliges the Greek poet to see the eternal meaning of all man's acts and destinies, to find them their place in a general scheme of the world, and to measure them by the loftiest religious and moral standards."[4]

Morris, in *The Earthly Paradise*, expresses in tentative form his

[3] For which see Dorothy M. Hoare, *The Works of Morris and of Yeats in Relation to Early Saga Literature* (1937; rpt. New York, 1971), pp. 50–76.

[4] Scholes and Kellogg, *The Nature of Narrative* (Oxford, 1966), pp. 36–37; Jaeger, *Paideia: The Ideals of Greek Culture*, trans. Gilbert Highet, 2d ed., I (New York, 1945), 43, 52.

sense of the "eternal meaning of all man's acts and destinies." In *The Life and Death of Jason* and *Sigurd the Volsung* this sense becomes something more akin to thought, a more consistent and discernible view of the "general scheme of the world." Further, while the "message" of *The Earthly Paradise* must be inferred, the Morrisian point of view is more apparent in *Jason*. Thus Lloyd Wendell Eshleman could interpret *Jason* as advocating "*the necessity of love of work, and of struggle in a just cause*, and *unwillingness to seek the easy and materialistic paradise of idle dreamers*."[5] From this stoic message to the overt social doctrines most critics have seen in *Sigurd the Volsung* it is a short step. But our concern is with the uniformity of vision in all three works and, indeed, in all Morris's writings.

Though *Jason* and *Sigurd* evince the same ontological point of view as that which informs *The Earthly Paradise*, what is there conceived spatially, or geographically, is in the epics apprehended in terms of time. The paradise-otherworld pattern that is a major ordering principle in *The Earthly Paradise* is transmuted in *Jason* and *Sigurd* into analogous cyclical patterns of human life that reflect symbolically the passing of the ages. Not that the paradise topos with all its associations is absent from the epic poems. On the contrary, both poems conform significantly to the patterns we have already noticed in *The Earthly Paradise*. The heroes of both poems must overcome monsters, and in both the heroes marry supernatural women whom they subsequently betray or forget, thus bringing doom on themselves. The otherworld in *Jason* is represented by the kingdom of Colchis, which is like an "earthly Paradise" to the Argonauts (II, 99), reached through magical flight or perilous voyage, where Medea is a princess possessing occult powers derived from the three-formed Hecate. The Symplegades, through which Jason and the Argonauts must pass, are the classic instance of the difficulties of passage to the otherworld, that is, to a transcendent state of existence.[6] Other paradise motifs appear as temptations to the mariners, such as the undersea world of the Sirens and the garden of the Hesperides. In *Sigurd* the fire-ringed mountain of Hindfell, where Sigurd finds the Valkyrie Brynhild, is clearly an otherworld manifestation, as Brynhild herself is quite frankly a supernatural being, at least in the first part of the narrative (Valkyries were traditionally associated

---

[5] *A Victorian Rebel: The Life of William Morris* (New York, 1940; reissued in London, 1943, as *William Morris: Prophet of England's New Order* under author's name of Lloyd Eric Grey), p. 104 (italics original). The 1940 edition has been reissued in a photographic reprint (New York, 1971) under original title and author's name.

[6] See Mircea Eliade, *Birth and Rebirth: The Religious Meanings of Initiation in Human Culture*, trans. Willard R. Trask (New York, 1958), pp. 65–66.

with swan maidens and the Norns).[7] Earlier in the poem, the scene of Fafnir's slaying, a desert wasteland "More changeless than mid-ocean," reached after a ride through a blackness like "the daylight of Hell, or the night of the doorway of God" (XII, 107–8), is an appropriate otherworld locale for the ultimate heroic deed, and Sigurd's ability to understand the language of the birds following his tasting of Fafnir's blood and flesh is, in Mircea Eliade's phrase, a " 'paradisial' syndrome."[8] The hero's relationship to society is clear in both poems. The people hail Jason's return to Iolchis as a return of the golden age:

> "Be thou our king—be thou our king alone,
> That we may think the age of iron gone,
> And Saturn come with every peaceful thing:—
> Jason for king! the Conqueror for king!"
>
> [II, 255]

And so Sigurd, the straightener of the crooked, is regarded universally as the hero who will bring in the millennium, as he is hailed in paraphrases of Isaiah:

And they sing of the golden Sigurd and the face without a foe,
And the lowly man exalted and the mighty brought alow.

    . . . . .

And glad is the poor in the Doom-ring when he seeth his face mid the Kings,
For the tangle straighteneth before him, and the maze of crookèd things.

[XII, 158, 182]

But *Jason* and *Sigurd* are not merely extended versions of similar tales from *The Earthly Paradise*. Their lengthiness makes it possible for Morris to develop themes of change and decline by exploring in leisurely fashion cyclical patterns within the lives of the heroes.

[7] Jacob Grimm, *Teutonic Mythology*, trans. James Steven Stallybrass, I (1883; rpt. New York, 1966), 417 ff. See also John Arnott MacCulloch, *The Mythology of All Races*, Vol. II, *Eddic* (Boston, 1930), pp. 260–61.

[8] "The Yearning for Paradise in Primitive Tradition," in *Myth and Mythmaking*, ed. Henry A. Murray (New York, 1960), p. 65.

Chapter IV

Jason and the Argo: The Limits of Mortality

FROM THE STANDPOINT of the heroic tradition, the character of Jason is interestingly equivocal, and Euripides made the most of this ironic ambiguity in his *Medea*. Morris's epic treatment of the story, though it does not deepen our psychological insights, amplifies the significance of the legend in another way, by relating the story of Jason to the greater subsuming patterns of destiny. The actions of the hero's life are so enmeshed in the coils of shifting ages as to render character a function of time itself, for Morris's narrative method in *The Life and Death of Jason* is to postulate a background of changing ages and then to show the cyclical relationship of events within the present age. But first let us consider the manner in which Morris has depicted his protagonist.

In Jason we have a hero who fails, in several important ways, to command our respect. We see him throughout the poem quite willing to depend upon Medea's machinations for the success of his enterprise, and then in later years unforgivably quick to put her aside for a younger woman who can better pamper his ego. So much is fixed by tradition, but Morris chose to emphasize Jason's shortcomings by treating Medea in a highly sympathetic manner. Here she is not the strange and barbaric foreign witch of Apollonius Rhodius, who followed Greek tradition in his characterization; Morris's heroine, like the Medea of Valerius Flaccus, is a beautiful and gentle maiden with magical powers. Morris omits the gruesome episode of Absyrtus' murder and dismemberment at his sister's hands; his Medea is in no way guilty of her brother's death, which indeed, occurring in combat with Jason, is comparatively honorable, considering that they are fighting over what is, after all, stolen goods. Most important, by including the downfall and death of Jason, brought about by his own betrayal of Medea, Morris provides a larger framework within which to consider the meaning of the Argonauts' quest. For the legend of Jason is structurally a series of betrayals; Morris, like other epic poets before him, makes the most of such natural unity with judicious and well-placed digressions and, further, conveys his concept of the circular nature of life and reality by emphasizing the intertwining connections among these betrayals.

The complex and subtle relationships between events of the past and the present are suggested throughout *Jason* much in the manner of Aeschylus' *Agamemnon*, in which the full significance of Agamemnon's death as the fulfillment of the curse of the House of Atreus is realized through reiterated references to the child sacrifices of past generations. Morris balances and prepares for the central betrayal of Medea by including in flashbacks the background story of how the golden fleece came to be in Colchis. Athamas' putting aside of his wife Nephele in order to marry Ino is a close parallel to Jason's rejection of Medea for Glauce. It is also, of course, an important part of the story of the golden fleece, as it explains why Phryxus and Helle, the children of Athamas and Nephele, were forced to flee to Colchis on the golden ram. But there is an ironic difference: Nephele is not motivated by revenge and accepts her unhappy lot, saving her children from the machinations of the avaricious Ino by arranging their flight on the ram, while Medea kills her children and, although Morris does not include her escape in his poem, herself finds asylum in Athens by magical flight. A further reverberation of the cruel stepmother motif occurs in the background history of Pelias himself, who, with his brother, had originally angered Juno by slaying his own mother's wicked stepmother, Sidero, within the sanctuary of the goddess. It is this deed that causes Juno to champion Jason against Pelias. Thus betrayal and its obverse, loyalty, are the crucial motivations governing the actions of the characters in *Jason*.

Treachery is reiterated in the story of Pelias' betrayal of his brother Aeson, Jason's father, in order to gain the throne. So does King Aetes, Medea's father, betray Phryxus in order to get possession of the golden fleece. And, as Phryxus betrays and sacrifices the magical ram which had aided him in his escape from Athamas and Ino, Jason betrays Medea, who had with her magical powers helped him gain the fleece and escape from Aetes, her father. Medea betrays her father in helping Jason; but her most monstrous betrayal is the luring of Pelias to death by dismemberment at the hands of his daughters (particularly ironic when we remember how Pelias began the chain of events that was to culminate in his own undoing by avenging his own parent). Pelias' suggestion to Jason that he go on the quest for the fleece is, of course, a treacherous one—Pelias believes the task to be impossible, and, as we have noticed, Jason betrays his responsibility to his father Aeson in accepting the quest.

Despite his instruction by the centaur Chiron both in the ways of nature and in his own family history, Jason fails throughout to realize either the full possibilities or the limitations of his own role in the developing pattern of events. Blinded by his naive egoism, and seemingly unconscious of the significance of Fate in the working out of human events, he sees no irony in accepting the fruits of Medea's labors (and her arranging of Pelias' murder by his daughters is for herself a spiritually costly act, as Morris makes clear), and, though hailed as a redeeming king upon his return to Iolchis, he is content to give up, within only ten years, the responsibilities of his throne for a life of pleasure. In other words, Jason accepts without question the help of others, but fails to discharge his own obligations to others, whether wife or subject. We might infer that Jason's obtuse egoism is what makes his heroic quest essentially superficial, for it fails to realize the underlying principles of cause and effect tying together past, present, and future (Necessity) or obligation and justice (*Dike*). This idea is implicit in the symbolism of the ship *Argo* (associated with the characteristically male rational ego) plowing the waves of the "conquered" sea, or deeper and dimly perceived forces of the cosmos (associated with the characteristically female generative instinctive urges).

It is useful here to recall that the voyage of the *Argo*, though given several different routes in classical sources, was generally thought to have encompassed the limits of the then known world. It was the notable pioneering nautical adventure of Greek legend, and in it we perceive an analogy with the so-called Orphic cosmogony, which is referred to by Apollonius Rhodius as he describes the song of Orpheus in his *Argonautica*: "He sang that Earth and Heaven and Sea formerly were fitted together into one form, and separated through destructive Hate."[1] The quest for the golden fleece, the culmination of generations of hatred and vengeance, can be seen as the quintessential act of conscious will that both defines and limits Earth, or the world of man, separating it from both Heaven (the spiritual realm of immortality) and the Sea (the unknown, chaotic, or primitive life of unconscious instinct). This heroic quest, then, becomes a type of the divisive act of creation, in which man in his intelligent navigation of the unformed void creates the limits of his own mortality.

Within this cosmogonical context, the contest between Orpheus and the Sirens in Book 14 takes on new significance. Their alternated songs are rival arguments for sea and land respectively. The Sirens sing the attractions of unchanging death beneath the waves, and our ears hear resonances of Tennyson's theme of the seductions of regressive sensuality and sleep. Orpheus, on the other hand, sings of the changing seasons, the cyclic patterns of human life in the kingdoms of the land. The lure of the Sirens is too much for Butes to resist, but

---

[1] From Kathleen Freeman, *Ancilla to the Pre–Socratic Philosophers* (Cambridge, Mass., 1962), p. 4.

Jason is not yet to be tempted. Much later, however, Medea's dream of the sea's revenge (II, 221) will prove to have been prophetic, when Jason, having renounced his throne and its responsibilities, succumbs to the compulsions of an aging sensualist to return symbolically to a paradisaical interlude in time, his youth, by wedding the adoring Glauce. For the past cannot be recaptured; it can only be affirmed and fulfilled by submission to the demands of the present (which in turn lead into the future). Jason's letter to Medea begging her to release him is a measure of the depth of his self-deception, for even while he accuses her of not letting the "old days" go, of not accepting change, he immediately reveals that he intends a psychological return to that period of his life preceding his acceptance of the quest—to a time when striving was unnecessary (II, 279–80). Recalling the regressive Prometheanism of the wanderers of *The Earthly Paradise*, Jason's renunciation of heroism for eroticism, the quest for a bower of bliss, must necessarily fail.

On the other hand, there are aspects of the quest for the golden fleece that make us question its validity as an act of heroism. The pagan hero, unlike the Christian saint, who seeks heavenly immortality through martyrdom, knows that death is final and inescapable, and can hope for immortality only in fame after death through great deeds. Thus the Argonauts seek "Undying fame when fleeting life is past" (II, 36), and their quest for the golden fleece is truly a quest for the immortality of fame. Jason's motivation in undertaking the quest for the fleece is, like that of the wanderers, a quest for eternal life. Morris's poem makes it clear that Jason is tempted by *selfish* dreams of glory and falls in accepting the quest:

> Meanwhile in Jason's heart did thoughts arise,
> That brought the treacherous blood into his cheek,
> And he forgot his father, old and weak,
> Left 'twixt the fickle people of the land
> And wily Pelias. . . .
>
> [II, 35]

The quest for the fleece is selfish and unworthy because, arising from no larger consideration than personal whim, it is not for the betterment of society. Further, because the quest entails the forsaking of his father, it constitutes a repudiation of the past and its claims; hence we see that Jason's unheroic tendencies at the close of his career are already inherent in the young "hero."

Theseus, the ideal ruler and most revered of Greek heroes, whom Morris includes among the Argonauts, contrary to precedent, illustrates by contrast what Jason's shortcomings are. Ironically, Jason

muses on Theseus' continuing exploits against the Minotaur and the
Amazons even while he himself awaits unknowing sleep and death
beneath the stem of the rotting *Argo*. Because the stem of the *Argo* has
supernatural associations, even oracular powers, Jason's death beneath its crushing weight is fraught with meaning. The manner of his
death was implicit in the nature of his quest. His end lay in his
beginning. This stem was the same post Argus was advised by Juno to
make into the ship's prow, "For soothly from Dodona doth it come, /
Though men forget it, the grey pigeons' home" (II, 40). Now, Dodona
was the site of an oracle and a sanctuary of Zeus. There a dove first
spoke to reveal the sanctity of the sacred oak with which it was
associated, and in later times priestesses operating the oracle were
referred to as doves.[2] Morris has emphasized, throughout *Jason*, the
all-encompassing power of Fate by calling attention to the prophecy
of the "half-shod man," for which Pelias sent to Dodona "where the
doves / Amid the oak-trees murmur of their loves" (II, 7). The oracular
properties of these birds are centrally important in the plot when
Jason must rely upon the help of the dove given him by Phineus to
navigate the Symplegades. Doves are also associated with the supernatural women, Medea and Circe. In Colchis, Aetes' marble house
stands silent, "Brushed round by doves" (II, 97), and Medea, visiting
Circe, passes "underneath the moaning of the dove" (II, 183). The
incessant moaning and murmuring of all these mysteriously pre-
scient doves is, then, a recurrent motif of the poem, punctuating the
tale of Jason's upward path to immortal fame with reminders that his
downfall must follow. When that downfall begins, its relationship to
previous events is suggested by the dove imagery. He first meets
Glauce at the temple of Citheraea, where "the grey-winged dove /
Hung crooning o'er his wrongs" and the doves "'mid the pillars
murmured of their loves" (II, 276). Glauce herself is depicted as a
dove; innocent and simple, in her prayer to Venus she also murmurs
(II, 277). She trembles "like some snow-trapped dove" when declaring
her love to Jason (II, 278), and on her wedding day arises and murmurs "words of joy and love, / No louder than the grey pink-footed
dove" (II, 287). Like a temple dove, she is sacrificed by burning. Thus
the dovelike Glauce, who brings Jason's destruction upon him, recalls
and parallels the dove of Phineus that aids Jason in his quest. Perigee
becomes atonement for apogee. We might paraphrase some lines
from Eliot's "Little Gidding" and say that the end of all Jason's
exploring was to arrive where he started.[3]

[2] *The Oxford Classical Dictionary*, 2d ed., ed. N. G. L. Hammond and H. H. Scullard
(Oxford, 1970), s.v. Dodona.
[3] T. S. Eliot, "Little Gidding," *Four Quartets* (New York, 1943), p. 39.

The meeting with Glauce brings the wheel of Jason's fortune full circle; this meeting is specifically related by Morris to Jason's meeting with Medea:

> when he saw her thus,
> The lapse of time seemed strange and piteous;
> For he bethought him of that other tide,
>
> . . . . .
>
> In King Aetes' hall; and when she drew
> Anigh unto him, back the past years flew,
> And he became that man entrapped again. . . .
>
> [II, 268]

Jason's fall comes about through his forgetting "past time" when he sees Glauce (II, 278), and his attempt to regain an irresponsible youth finally results instead in a regression to infancy. In his ineffectual despair, he behaves like any Victorian child in Gathorne-Hardy's *Unnatural History of the Nanny*:

> Then with the crone did Jason go along,
> And let her thin hand hold his fingers strong,
> As though a child he were in that old day. . . .

His old nurse gives him a soothing drink, puts him to bed, pacifies him with confident prophecies, and he falls asleep, "While at his feet good watch the crone did keep" (II, 291).[4]

And so not only are the events of Jason's life the inevitable outgrowths of the deeds of past generations, they are also intrinsically related to other occurrences within his own lifetime, and thus the individual life span of the protagonist becomes a paradigm for all the cycles of human life. The tragedy of this particular hero arises from his ego-induced blindness, that is, his failure to perceive the subsuming patterns of destiny and to accommodate himself to them.

It is this Argo-ego that defines the limits of the Earth, or the mortal world. In creating the boundaries, or conditions, of human life, it separates mankind on one hand from the immortal forces, or gods, of Heaven, and on the other from the unconsciously regenerating womb of physical life, the Sea. If this is so, then it is one of the greatest ironies of an extremely ironic poem that we should be continually reminded by the narrator of the transience and consequent sadness of human life. For the hero's act of will, of which the narrator sings, is the very source of the narrator's sorrow. The song of the Hesperides in Book 14 makes this clear. Their garden is a vestige of the lost golden age, left "Unchanged, unchanging" only because the hero Hercules

---

[4] Jonathan Gathorne-Hardy, *The Unnatural History of the Nanny* (New York, 1973).

has not yet arrived to slay the guardian dragon and steal the golden apples (II, 210–11). When this happens, the Garden of the Hesperides too will become assimilated to the finite world of man and become subject to change. Then history, the record of change, will begin. In this connection it is suggestive that the northward voyage of the Argonauts after the capture of the fleece takes them through a paradigmatic evolutionary history of the changing earth, beginning with a battle with "worms," or primeval reptiles, and progressing through encounters with stone-age men who practice human sacrifice, to a skirmish with slightly more civilized barbarians. The stages of the voyage can be regarded as progressive phases of the history of the fallen world, where dragons can no longer live in harmony with beautiful maidens. In fact, the northward voyage of the Argonauts belongs not so much to the genre of fantasy and myth as it does to the time-travel genre of science fiction. These relatively realistic experiences follow immediately the escape of the Argonauts from the vengeful Aetes, suggesting that it is the audaciously egoistic theft of the fleece which sets in motion such Darwinian events quite out of the usual run of Greek myth.

Such a paradigm of history finds a corresponding symbol in the seaside temple where Medea stages the final scene of Pelias' murder. This "ancient fane" is "twofold." Its lower story, built with "Square marble pillars, huge, and red as blood," was once a temple to gods now completely forgotten. The upper story, built of "Fair slim white pillars set in goodly rows" is considerably less foreboding, but the gods to which it was dedicated are now little known (II, 241). The two stories of the fane obviously suggest successive chapters of religious history, from dark bloody rites below to the worship of beauty and intellect above. But the upper level is built upon the lower, and so corresponds to the rational mind, or ego, unmindful of the primeval gods, that is, the primitive forces that brought into being its foundations. These two levels further suggest the relationship of the Earth, that which is open to the light of day, or the intellect, to the Sea, that which is hidden beneath the surface of the waves. Pelias, son of Poseidon, is another aspect of the Sea conquered by Jason's Argo-ego.

On the level of plot, it is ironic that Pelias should be lured to his death by his longing for immortality, an eternal youth which would "bring again / The golden age" (II, 225), and it is even more ironic that Medea, herself superior to such a longing, should understand so well its power and know how to use it. She is the only main character of the poem who is beyond the temptations of eternal youth; she has even given up her own supernatural immortality by falling into the "troublous sea of love," as Circe terms it (II, 186). She longs for the

simplicity of mortal life "In homely places, where the children play, /
Who change like me, grow old, and die some day" (II, 209). Unlike
Jason, who looks backward, Medea is always aware of the "fearsome
future" (II, 174), even foreseeing his betrayal of her (II, 125). Medea's
charming of the dragon guarding the golden fleece may be considered
as emblematic of her power over Time, or Chronos, who, according to
the Orphic theogony as described by Damascius and Athenagoras,
was a serpent. To quote Damascius, this serpent, in addition to
"having the heads of a bull and a lion with the face of a god in
between" also "had wings, and was called Ageless Time. . . . With him
was united Necessity or Adrasteia, an element having no body, and
spread over the whole universe, fastening it together."[5] In effect,
Medea stays Time for Jason in order that he may steal the treasure
which will ensure the immortality of his name, but the demands of
Necessity, that element which binds together all of reality, past,
present, and future, must finally be triumphant. The witch Medea, a
forerunner of the benign witch figures of Morris's late romances, is in
tune with Necessity, the unseen but finally omnipotent motive force
of the cosmos, and it is therefore she who truly represents Morris's
ideal of heroism in *The Life and Death of Jason.*

[5] See Freeman, p. 3. There is no indication to my knowledge that Morris was aware of
the complex and enigmatic religious associations of Orpheus, who was not only to
become identified as the prophet of a mystery religion bearing his name but was to
become himself a type of the dying and resurrected god Dionysus and even a proto-
Christ; Morris's Orpheus is only the poet-magician who charms through his music. But
Morris must have noted in the *Argonautica* of Apollonius Rhodius that the songs
attributed to Orpheus are cosmogonical in theme, treating of the separation of Earth,
Heaven, and Sea and of the beginning of the rule of Time. Though the so-called Orphic
cosmogony is not actually a part of Morris's poem, some aspects of this complex of ideas
known as Orphism have provocative implications for an interpretation of *Jason.* See
W. K. C. Guthrie, *Orpheus and Greek Religion: A Study of the Orphic Movement* (New
York, 1966), pp. 69–147.

Chapter V

The Immolation of Sigurd:
Surpassing the Self

MORRIS'S TWO EPICS, as I have suggested, have many points of similarity. As both are treatments of traditional heroic subjects, this must necessarily be so. But *The Life and Death of Jason* and *The Story of Sigurd the Volsung and the Fall of the Niblungs* are, in a number of significant ways, profoundly different, and this difference may in large part be attributed to a basic difference between Greek and Norse myth. Morris has accomplished something of a tour de force in that he manages to emphasize not only the similarities but also the differences, thereby throwing the differences into relief, as it were, and so achieves much of the effect of *Sigurd* by startling us with the unexpected, not only in prosody, which, as everyone knows, is an attempt to suggest some of the qualities of the original sagas, but in the underlying mood of forbidding grandeur, which depends upon characterization and the selection of plot episodes from the source as well as upon diction and versification.

Even more forcibly than in *Jason*, Morris impresses upon us in *Sigurd the Volsung* that the world of the poem is a fallen one, that it was preceded by a lost golden age. The poem begins with a description of the Volsung dwelling as it was "ere the world was waxen old," when the unforgotten Gods "walked with men." But even in this paradisaical time there was foreknowledge of the final cataclysm, "the fading and the last of the latter days" (XII, 1). This, the Ragnarok, or Twilight of the Gods, has no counterpart in Greek myth. And so it is quite appropriate that, whereas we find cosmogonical themes in *Jason*, we find an apocalyptic motif in *Sigurd*. Further, all the characters in *Sigurd* are to some extent aware of the ineluctable approach of world conflagration (and, as we shall see, the best live their lives in a manner dictated by its implications) and so might be said to be future- or death-oriented, whereas all the characters in *Jason*, save Medea, seem to be past- or birth-oriented. This difference accounts for a basic difference in characterization in the two poems. There is no character in *Sigurd* who evidences any of the regressively infantile / erotic tendencies so noticeable in Jason or in some other characters of *The Earthly Paradise*. Morris has perceived a subtle yet profound and basic difference in ontological outlook and has conveyed it in his characterizations.

If *Sigurd* is a poem that looks forward to the transforming end of our world, we might ask why Morris has taken pains to remind us of the golden age, or the age of the Dwarfs, which preceded it, when "fair was the earth" (XII, 75), and, even before that, the stages of creation of which Gunnar sings in the serpent pit (XII, 297). The answer is that not only are we thus made to see that, as these previous ages ended, so must the present one, for even worlds "come and go" (XII, 81), but the perspective of vast aeons of time enables the poet to show the mystical coincidence of past and present, the inseparability of what has gone before and what is to come. "The end is where we start from."[1] So that Gunnar's death in Atli's snake pit recalls Sigurd's ambush of the "ash-grey Serpent" Fafnir, accomplished while lying in a gravelike pit in order to strike from beneath (II, 110–13). The serpent who kills Gunnar is the "Grey and Ancient," coming "of the kin of the Serpent once wrought all wrong to nurse, / The bond of earthly evil, the Midworld's ancient curse" (XII, 298). This apocalyptic serpent is the same one who gnaws at the root of Yggdrasil, the world tree of which the Branstock is a type; its success in killing the tree is to cause the final destruction of the universe supported by Yggdrasil. And so the victory of the "Grey and Ancient" over Gunnar is an intimation of the end, when Thor is to die by the venom of the Midgard Serpent. The interconnections of the serpent episodes illustrate Morris's method of unifying his long poem by analogous narrative incidents, here as in *Jason*.

As in *Jason*, many of these analogous narrative incidents in *Sigurd* hinge on betrayal, and in both poems the prevalence of treachery can be seen as an inevitable manifestation of a fallen world, where loyalty and honor are but short-lived. So the treacherous slaying of Sigurd is foreshadowed in the ambush of his father by a rival, and the betrayal of the Volsungs by Signy's husband, Siggeir, prefigures the betrayal of the Niblungs by Gudrun's husband Atli. Evil calls forth vengeance and purification, and so the fallen world proceeds inexorably toward Ragnarok: Signy's terrible revenge, in which she burns herself with her entire family, is echoed in Gudrun's burning of Atli in his hall before her suicide, itself foreshadowed in Brynhild's, and both holocausts are types of the final world conflagration that shall atone for all. Morris's inclusion of the early history of the Volsungs, for which he has been criticized, is in fact essential to his theme, which requires a larger frame of reference than the single lifetime of Sigurd, although within this single span we can see other motifs coming full cycle, the most striking example being the image of Sigurd's super-

[1] Eliot, "Little Gidding," *Four Quartets*, p. 38.

natural sword, the Wrath of Sigurd, lying between the corpses of
Sigurd and Brynhild on their funeral pyre, just as it lies between
them on the night when he weds her in the semblance of Gunnar.[2] The
difference in the meaning of the sword on these two occasions sums
up the meaning of their doomed love. The Wrath of Sigurd is the
hereditary gift of Odin to the Volsung line, representing their heroic
destiny, which cannot be altered, for, as Morris continually reminds
us, the Norns order all. Sigurd is the last of the Volsung line, a link
with the unfallen world, and his destiny in these latter days is to fall
prey to the base passions of lesser men. It is this destiny that requires
the love of Sigurd and Brynhild to burn unsatisfied until all is consumed by the fire of Ragnarok. Their funeral pyre, like their love, is
thus a type of the ultimate world fire in which their destinies are to be
united, and the sword of destiny linking them together on their pyre
becomes a symbol of their final union.

Now, the shape-changing episode when Sigurd actually changes
bodies with Gunnar in order to woo Brynhild for him is of central
importance. It is the final metamorphosis of a whole series, beginning
with Signy's changing bodies with a witch-wife in order that she may
dupe her brother Sigmund into incest and thereby perpetuate the
Volsung line. We again see a queen voluntarily assuming the guise of
an inferior when Hiordis changes place with her handmaid in order
to protect the life of the unborn Sigurd. More spectacular shape-
changes take place when Sigmund and Sinfiotli turn into wolves and
Fafnir becomes a dragon. Both wolves and dragons have apocalyptic
significance: Fenrir's Wolf, mentioned several times by Morris (XII,
21, 73, 144), is chained until Ragnarok, when he is to break loose,
devour the sun, and kill Odin (the other wolf, Moongarm, is to devour
the moon); we have already mentioned the Midgard Serpent, who is
destined to bring about the death of Thor at the same time. And so we
might see these shape-shiftings as yet another complex of anticipa-
tions of Ragnarok, for the final world convulsion is to change the
nature of reality forever. But there is another aspect to the shape-
changes, and it has its roots in the Norse concept of man's dual
nature. The spirit or soul was considered to be the gift of Odin,
whereas the physical body was thought to come from Loder, or Loke,
as he came to be called. Thus man's soul belongs to the spirit world, or
Heaven, and his body to the material world, or the Deep. These are
joined together in earthly life, to be separated at death, or the changing of one's life, in order to return to their original sources, either
Valhalla (Heaven) or Helheim (the Deep). There they will remain

[2] Mackail, I, 331.

until Ragnarok, the time when all temporary things will perish together—when all the dross will be consumed and the gold refined, to put it in another context.[3] Ragnarok can therefore be seen as the ultimate unifying event when all differences shall become nought in the cosmic transformation, the final changing of life. It is this aspect of Ragnarok as the ultimate union and transformation of all elements that is most important to an interpretation of *Sigurd the Volsung*.

Sigurd is remarkable for his dedication to the humble and downtrodden levels of society. Morris continually reminds us that Sigurd is the great leveler, by whose deeds is "the lowly man exalted and the mighty brought alow" (XII, 158). As Margaret R. Grennan points out, Morris's Sigurd is much more altruistic in his aims than the saga hero.[4] The point is that Sigurd is distinguished from all the other champions of Morris's epic by his larger vision, which takes in not only all levels of human society but extends beyond the earth itself to include all of reality. His great oath, spoken at the celebration of his marriage to Gudrun, is sworn "By the Earth," "by all the Earth's increase," "by the sun," "By the Salt-Sea-Flood," "By the Heavens and Stars." He ends: "So help me Earth and Heavens, and the Under-sky and Seas, / And the Stars in their ordered houses, and the Norns that order these!" (XII, 177–78). The various realms of Norse cosmology have shares in the making of the hero. The horse Greyfell is the gift of Odin, as is the reforged sword of Sigmund, the Wrath of Sigurd. But the sword, once thrust into the Branstock tree, symbol of the Volsung line and itself a metaphor for cosmic unity, must be reforged by the dwarf Regin. Odin's gifts bind Sigurd to Asgard; Regin's tutelage binds him to the underworld, for the dwarfs had their beginning beneath the surface of the earth.[5] The developing Sigurd thus subsumes within himself the quintessences of the

[3] See commentary by R. B. Anderson, *Norse Mythology*, 3d ed. (Chicago, 1879), pp. 391–97. The striking similarities between the Norse concept of Ragnarok and the Judeo-Christian apocalypse were apparent to Morris, who discounted the notion of Christian influence. In his lecture "The Early Literature of the North—Iceland," he argued that "one of the most vigorous branches of the most progressive race in the world" must have been able to "have a mythology developed by themselves" and that this mythology "seems rather to be derived from and coloured by the same dualism which overlaid the ancient nature-worship of the Persians, and formed the very long-lived religion still maintained by the Parsees" (Lemire, p. 190). On the problematical nature of determining the extent of Christian influence on Norse apocalyptic concepts, see MacCulloch, p. 342.

[4] *William Morris: Medievalist and Revolutionary* (New York, 1945), p. 43.

[5] See *The Prose Edda of Snorri Sturluson: Tales from Norse Mythology*, trans. Jean I. Young (Berkeley and Los Angeles: Univ. of California Press, 1971), p. 41: "Then the gods . . . remembered how dwarfs had quickened in the earth and under the soil like maggots in flesh. . . . by the decree of the gods they acquired human understanding and the appearance of men, although they lived in the earth and in rocks."

various realms of the cosmos and so becomes in himself an emblem of cosmic unity. On the human level, his death is tragic, though inevitable; on the metaphysical level, his individual death and funeral pyre prefigure that stupendous catastrophe that shall unite all in destruction and bring forth a new creation.

The dark, "swart-haired" Niblungs (XII, 160, 175), in contrast to the golden Sigurd's selfless altruism, exhibit a hubristic desire to take the earth for themselves; they look forward to the time "When all the world of glory shall be called the Niblungs' home" (XII, 156). Their limited vision extends only to personal or family glory and honor. This selfish egoism, focused in Grimhild, finds expression in her plotting to confine and assimilate the superhuman heroism of both Sigurd and Brynhild for her own family. When Sigurd takes on the shape of Gunnar, he literally becomes less than his true self. In diminishing his being, he is beguiled by the witchery of Grimhild, which represents the limiting and blinding influence of personal egoism. Sigurd's inexplicable sorrow after drinking Grimhild's potion is a subliminal recognition of his bondage to a lesser vision. The Fall of the Niblungs proceeds from their failure to transcend the limitations of the self, and their fall is complete in the shameful alliance with Atli, which, motivated by greed for his kingdom, literally marries them with avarice and lust. Even so, Morris's characterization does not deprive them of their humanity, and the heroic death struggle of Gunnar and Hogni in Atli's hall redeems them from their complicity in the murder of Sigurd. The Niblungs' joy in rushing toward certain death makes us think that they have at last learned to emulate Sigurd, to look forward and embrace the coming final destruction. Their unequivocally heroic deaths show that, for them, Sigurd has become not only a hero but a prophet of the Ragnarok.

Sigurd may properly be considered a prophet because his words and deeds constitute a guide for mankind in a cosmos where all is ordered by the Norns, or the forces of destiny. As Brynhild says, without man's helping, "shall no whit of their will befall." The very sun responds to man's acquiescence in the cosmic plan:

> "And the way of the sun is tangled, it is wrought of the dastard's lack.
> But the day when the fair earth blossoms, and the sun is bright above,
> Of the daring deeds is it fashioned. . . .

[XII, 126]

The sense here is that the working of the universe depends upon the deeds of man, and so the reiterated identification of Sigurd with the sun is something more in this poem than the traditional analogy. Further, Sigurd's vows to Brynhild refer to the sun's dying (XII, 130,

147); this is not only a tragically ironic reference to his own death but suggests his awareness that even this form of the universe, intimately associated with his own being, will pass away like those that preceded it.

The attractively dramatic image of the dying sun may be the reason Morris chose to use the traditional masculine association for the sun, although in Norse mythology the sun is female and the moon male, for he could hardly characterize Sigurd as a dying moon. In this matter he had the further impetus of Max Müller's famous "solar-myth" theory. In his article "Bellerophon," written in 1855, the renowned philologist and mythologist of Oxford "proves" by his philological method that Bellerophon's name had "a meaning analogous to that of other names of solar heroes, the enemies of the dark powers of nature, whether in the shape of night, or dark clouds or winter," and he discusses Sigurd as a solar hero in his "Comparative Mythology" of 1856. Müller would have Brynhild, "like the spring after the sleep of winter, brought back to new life by the love of Sigurd," only to be carried away by Gunnar, "darkness." There is much in *Sigurd*, as, for that matter, in *Jason* and *The Earthly Paradise*, to suggest that Morris was influenced, aesthetically if not philosophically, by Müller's theory or a similar one: the darkness of the Niblungs is constantly contrasted to Sigurd's brightness; they are the "Cloudy People," and Gudrun's hair is like a dark cloud, falling "down behind her like a cloak of the sweet-breathed night" (XII, 134, 200, 201, 306). Brynhild, on the contrary, is bright and fair like Sigurd. However, in the awakening scene, she is described in terms of the moon. She is a "pale grey image," which "gleameth in the morn." Sigurd's effect on the virgin shield maiden is like that of the rising sun on the waning moon in the dawn of their meeting (XII, 122–24). The overcoming of the cold and sterile moon by the fertile warmth of the rising sun is a symbolic sex act, intrinsically related to the fructifying deed of heroism with which it is associated. But their meeting is even more significant on the level of cosmological symbolism for, as Joseph Campbell, speaking of the "pagan religious disciplines," points out, the "image of the 'Meeting of Sun and Moon' is everywhere symbolic" of the "realization of an identity *in esse* of the individual (microcosm) and the universe (macrocosm), which, when achieved, would bring together in one order of act and realization the principles of eternity and time, . . . male and female." In other words, the meeting of Sigurd and Brynhild on Hindfell, when solar and lunar cycles coincide, foreshadows the culmination of time and the melding of individual identities in the universal conflagration.[6]

[6] *Prose Edda*, p. 38; both "Bellerophon" and "Comparative Mythology" are printed in

Another and simpler meaning of the sun imagery is that Sigurd's life is analogous to the rising and falling sun and the fleeting triumph of his career is as a single day in the vast cycle of the ages. By extension, Sigurd's brief life is symbolic of the life of man, who must "tread the endless circle" (XII, 104), seeking only the satisfaction of having done well his fated part. This is the burden of Sigurd's answer to Regin when he speaks of man's brief life:

> "Fare forth, O glorious sun;
> Bright end from bright beginning, and the mid-way good to tell,
> And death, and deeds accomplished, and all remembered well!"
>
> [XII, 104]

Morris's fascination with the great hero of the Teutonic world marks him as a man intensely alive to the intellectual currents of his time. In the following chapter we shall consider some of the deeper philosophical implications of Morris's "Teutonism"; here we note simply that his interest in heroes, especially Germanic ones, was quite natural in a young writer of the generation following Carlyle's and that his developing enthusiasm for things Gothic, as opposed to Roman, was consonant with a general nationalistic fervor gathering force in England, as elsewhere, during the nineteenth century (although Kipling, among others, entertained a pro-imperialist admiration of Rome). But a number of passages in *Sigurd the Volsung* suggest a relevance to yet another nineteenth-century phenomenon, Marxism. The argument for interpreting *Sigurd* as an indication of Morris's "coming espousal of the socialistic cause" is usually based on the frequent references in the poem to the Ragnarok, which is thought to have been related in Morris's mind to the world revolution predicted by the Marxists, and on the many descriptions of Sigurd as a champion of the people.[7] But, though its implications may approach or even parallel socialist revolutionary doctrines, *Sigurd* is not a socialist poem. Its very concentration on the deeds of the hero makes it foreign to Marxist ideology. Kenelm Burridge, discussing Marxism within the context of millenarianism, remarks that Marxist sociology cannot explain the prophet, or hero, and his inspiration: "Positive and materialist, it prefers to regard the prophet as irrelevant, accidental, or at most as occupying a socially determined role, an ambiguous and unnecessary catalyst in a developmental process that might be more rationally achieved and ordered without him."[8] In

---

Chips from a German Workshop, II (New York, 1870), 1–141, and 170–86 (quoted passages are from pp. 108 and 179); Campbell, *Masks of God: Occidental Mythology*, pp. 163–64.

[7] See Robert W. Gutman, Introduction, *Volsunga Saga*, trans. William Morris (New York: Collier Books, 1962), p. 70.

[8] *New Heaven, New Earth: A Study of Millenarian Activities* (New York, 1969), p. 131.

any case, Morris, who did not read Marx until 1883, was probably more or less ignorant of the finer points of socialist theory when he joined the Democratic Federation in that year. And Eshleman has shown, from the evidence of a number of Morris's speeches and essays, that Morris's "profound philosophy" preceded his joining of the federation by several years. Whether profound or not, Morris's developing world view was certainly traditional. Bernard Wall has expressed it well:

The longing for the perfect terrestrial society is much older and stabler than Marxian economics. History seems to show that, whatever the reason for it, this longing is implanted in us all. It is bound up with that desire for bettering and perfecting all things which man experiences as man. In some ages it has taken the form of a nostalgia for the past: the Jews, the Greeks, and the Romans all had their story of the golden age.[9]

But aside from the whole question of Morris's knowledge of Marxist theory, we have shown that the basic ideas underlying *Sigurd*, which May Morris terms the "central work" of her father's life (XII, xxiii), are not significantly different from those found in *Jason* and *The Earthly Paradise*. The true importance of Morris's socialism in a consideration of his life's work, then, is not that his thinking was influenced by the socialist movement but that the socialist movement came to hand ready-made as a most appropriate and timely embodiment of his deepest compulsions, a means of putting into practice those ideals he had come to believe in. Morris's political activism, far from being a schizoid departure from an escapist poetic philosophy, was a practical application of the world view informing his poetry, his way of emulating the great heroes of his poems, whose lives and deeds attest the efficacy, the divine sanction, of action. His poems, advocating as they do the stoic acceptance of the call to heroism, were realized in his own life if in no one else's.

[9] Hulse, p. 79; Eshleman, pp. 185–86; Wall, "William Morris and Karl Marx," *Dublin Review*, 202, No. 404 (Jan. 1938), 40. On the traditional nature of Marx's apocalyptic view of history, see also Abrams, pp. 313 ff.

Part Three
From Romantic Visions
to Visionary Romance

Introduction to Part Three

THE ONE MORRIS volume that has enjoyed a steadily increasing critical acclaim since its publication in 1858 is *The Defence of Guenevere and Other Poems*. It has not often been suggested that there are any significant points of similarity between these early poems and the later narrative poems and romances; on the contrary, it is often noted that the excellence of *The Defence of Guenevere* lies in its unlikeness to Morris's other writings, that is, in the originality of its startlingly blunt and economical style, a style Morris abandoned in his later writings. It has also been observed that Morris's depiction of the brutality and violence of the Middle Ages in this volume of verse is unlike anything else written in the nineteenth century; Cecil Lang suggests, revising a statement by Ronald Fuller, that Morris's poetry "came nearer the 'courage and cruelty of the Middle Ages' than any poetry written in any century preceding, including the Middle Ages." It is evident from the biographical material available that Morris was able to accomplish this because he was possessed of a profound and ingrained, almost instinctive, knowledge of the customs and manners of medieval life. May Morris writes: "He never looked upon himself as an archaeologist, yet his knowledge of the everyday usages of past times was amazing; it was an instinct, a sort of second sight" (I, xvi). This knowledge grew naturally and inexorably from childhood interests; as his biographers relate, the young Morris had read all the novels of Scott by the age of seven, and, as a child, rode about in the area of Epping Forest clad in a miniature suit of armor.[1]

It is not surprising then that the two major sources for the poems of *The Defence of Guenevere* were Malory and Froissart, the most prominent chroniclers of medieval fact and fancy. But only six of the thirty poems included in the volume are actually based on the Arthurian cycle, whereas all thirty poems demonstrate the youthful poet's encyclopedic understanding of the medieval world, whether or not directly inspired by Froissart or other sources. My point is that the

[1] Lang further suggests that the real significance of *The Defence of Guenevere* is that, in these poems, "Morris demonstrated how verse could be both poetic and brutal" (*The Pre-Raphaelites and Their Circle*, 2d ed. [Chicago: Univ. of Chicago Press, 1975], p. 508, referring to *William Morris*, ed. Ronald Fuller [Oxford, 1956], p. 39); Henderson, p. 6.

terse realism of the *Guenevere* poems is directly related to Morris's acute sense of history. This is what, at least in part, stylistically differentiates his poetry from Rossetti's, which sprang rather from literary tradition. Although Morris was adept in intricate and traditional verse forms, his early poetry does not bring to mind any specific literary progenitors as do, for instance, Swinburne's classically inspired poetry or Rossetti's sonnets, which recall so clearly the love sonnets of Petrarch and, especially, Dante. Morris also wrote conventional medievalized love lyrics, but these are not the most memorable poems of the volume. The tough realism of such poems as "Sir Peter Harpdon's End," "Concerning Geffray Teste Noire," and, of course, "The Haystack in the Floods" comes from no literary model—not even Browning, whose style Morris acknowledged his own resembled somewhat, wrote anything quite like these poems (and certainly Chaucer did not).[2] Though Morris's Malory poems are doubtless to some extent the fruitage of his boyhood inspiration by Tennyson's Arthurian poems, it is worth noting that before 1858 Tennyson had published only "Morte d'Arthur" and "The Lady of Shalott." Kathleen Tillotson has reminded modern readers of Tennyson's originality and artistic daring in venturing upon a new and theretofore unacceptable subject for poetry;[3] while Morris followed Tennyson's lead in treating the Matter of Britain, it was still very much a venture into uncharted literary territory. And Morris did not slavishly accept the Tennysonian vision of that legendary world, but tended, in these youthful poems, toward a euhemeristic interpretation of legendary events: in his "Near Avalon," Arthur is, plausibly if anticlimactically, buried in Glastonbury rather than wafted to Avalon.

Nor did Morris ignore history during the period of writing *The Life and Death of Jason* and *The Earthly Paradise*, though these works were in the main inspired by myth and legend. The latter work is set in a specific historical framework, and the wanderers of the frame story sail from medieval Europe to recognizable geographical regions of the pre-Columbian New World in their doomed quest. Even the traditionally fabulous return voyage of the Argonauts is envisaged in a recognizable prehistoric Europe, though Morris did not seem to have troubled himself overmuch with geographical accuracy.[4]

And Morris was fascinated with the actuality of the events recorded

---

[2] Mackail, I, 132.

[3] "Tennyson's Serial Poem," in Geoffrey and Kathleen Tillotson, *Mid-Victorian Studies* (London, 1965), pp. 82–85.

[4] When pressed, Morris said the Argonauts "probably went north by the Don or the Dvina and came out by the Vistula" (*Works*, II, xxiv).

in the Icelandic sagas that he began reading and translating in the late sixties. One has only to read his accounts of his two trips to Iceland to appreciate this fact; throughout these physically arduous experiences Morris never tired of viewing the landscapes through which he passed in relation to the legendary and historical events associated with them. He had, of course, for some time been reading the heroic literature of the Germanic peoples as the history of the race. As he wrote in the preface to his translation of *The Volsunga Saga*: "For this is the Great Story of the North, which should be to all our race what the Tale of Troy was to the Greeks—to all our race first, and afterwards, when the change of the world has made our race nothing more than a name of what has been—a story too—then should it be to those that come after us no less than the Tale of Troy has been to us" (VII, 286).

There was in fact a general enthusiasm in the latter half of the nineteenth century for seeking historical verification for a number of literary classics, not to mention the Bible. Schliemann's thoroughly self-publicized excavations at Troy, for instance, were undertaken with the express purpose of verifying the events and locale of the *Iliad*, which Morris had himself begun to translate. Morris, interested as he was in archaeology, must certainly have been keenly interested in Schliemann's discoveries and their implications for the Homeric epics. At any rate, Morris's deep preoccupation with the Icelandic sagas—the epics of the north—seems to have effected a synthesis in his mind between history and heroic literature. Fortunately, he resisted the temptation (if it existed) to indulge in mere euhemerism; rather, his growing apprehension of the hero as a figure of destiny clearly out of the ordinary run of mankind enabled him, in the last ten years of his life, to begin a new phase of his literary career with the creation of a new genre—which has never been satisfactorily named but might be called the "heroic prose romance"—on a firm base of historical veracity.

Chapter VI

The Uses of History:
The Healing of the Nations

ALTHOUGH *A Dream of John Ball* is not properly a prose romance (it is rather more like a combination of *Past and Present* and *Piers Plowman*), it was the first significant work in prose undertaken by Morris in his mature years and seems to have started him in this new direction, being followed shortly by *The House of the Wolfings* and *The Roots of the Mountains. John Ball*, based on the 1381 Peasants' Revolt in Kent, seems to have been rather well received in its day and still enjoys a respectable critical acclaim. It is often praised for its simplicity and lucidity, and indeed it is admirably straightforward in accomplishing its purpose of arousing a consciousness of the historical evolution of freedom from tyranny, a freedom that the Dreamer, Morris, can only anticipate as he awakens to Victorian London. It was, as is well known, written as an expression of the socialist political convictions he held at that period, and the final chapters, tracing the course of economic development in England from the fourteenth century to the nineteenth, present, as may be expected, a Marxist view. Nonetheless, *John Ball* seems to represent the beginning of Morris's prose romances and, further, a beginning deeply rooted in the actual history of England. The English Peasants' Revolt was an event of considerable importance in the development of modern social thought, and it is characteristic of Morris that he should have been drawn to such a subject. Norman Cohn, in his *Pursuit of the Millennium*, sees in the pronouncements attributed to John Ball by the chroniclers Froissart and Walsingham the first recorded expression of millenarianism, that is, the belief that the entire earth is imminently to be transformed into an egalitarian paradise—in short, a utopia.[1] If John Ball's famous sermon was indeed the first postulation of a golden age to come, it truly marked a revolution in thinking, perhaps the most significant in the history of modern thought.

In his next volume, *The House of the Wolfings*, Morris encompassed an even broader historical viewpoint and took for his subject what his daughter would call "the world-history that was enacted in the Plains and among the Great Mountains of mid-Europe" (XVII, xiv–xv). Since May Morris pointed out a number of years ago that *The Wolfings*

[1] *The Pursuit of the Millennium* (London, 1957), pp. 209–11.

and *The Roots* are seen historically as opposed to the later romances, which "lead us straight into the radiance of fairy-land" (XIV, xxv), it is hardly iconoclastic to emphasize this historicity. Morris's venture into this new genre, whether it be called romance, heroic fantasy, or whatever, was occasioned from the beginning by a strong consciousness of what was actual in the past, and, parallel to this, a strong desire to influence an actual future.

The House of the Wolfings (1888) is an illuminating introduction to the prose romances of Morris's mature years, not only because it was the first of the series, but also because it illustrates the major themes and patterns of these romances, showing clearly their origins in the sagas and epics that Morris had been translating in the preceding decades. Perhaps because it is an early essay in a new form, it also shows most obviously what have often been anathematized as weaknesses of Morris's romances (or of his work in general). In short, *The House of the Wolfings* is not the best of the romances, nor even one of the most interesting, but, as intellectual topography, it allows us to chart where Morris had been and where he was going. In this, the first of the mature romances, he deals with a historically recognizable, and, more important, a historically significant subject, clearly fixed in the time and space of this world (though hardly with excessive exactitude), and, because of its national (in the largest sense of the word) importance, worthy of epic treatment. The locale, not named by Morris, is one of the forested areas north of the Danube (also not named) inhabited by the Goths during the early years of the Roman Empire. May Morris refers to this region as the "wonderful land about the foot of the Italian Alps," by which Morris was fascinated (XIV, xxv). The time is deliberately inexact, but Morris tells us at the end of the tale that the Romans began about that period to "stay the spreading of their dominion, or even to draw in its boundaries somewhat" (XIV, 208). The tale concerns a Gothic tribe, the Men of the Mark, and their successful defense against Roman invasion of their homeland, situated in a great wooded plain. Morris's central theme is thus the triumph of liberty over tyrannical forces—a theme common to most of his romances.

Morris's tale is a work of fiction, something like a historical novel, and it would therefore be pointless to seek an exact historical source for it. (Morris reacted with explosive scorn when a German professor, impressed with the realistic details of Morris's description of Germanic tribal life, questioned him about the Mark;[2] May Morris,

[2] Morris's typically explosive reaction to the professor's request is mentioned in H. Halliday Sparling, *The Kelmscott Press and William Morris, Master–Craftsman* (London, 1924), p. 50.

describing the incident, remarks that the poet "sometimes dreamed realities without having documentary evidence of them" [XIV, xxv].) Nevertheless, the setting as well as the circumstances of the battle between the Romans and the Men of the Mark suggest that Morris may have been inspired in part by the famous Battle of the Teutoburg Forest, an incident of surpassing importance in the development of German nationalism and, by extension, "Aryan" consciousness (and Morris, as we shall see, was very much caught up in the great nineteenth-century tide of enthusiasm for the "Aryan" tradition).[3] This famous battle, often credited with preventing Rome from conquering Germany, took place A.D. 9; it is well known that Caesar Augustus was haunted thereafter by the memory of this military disaster that occurred when Arminius, a prince of the Cherusci (though actually a Roman citizen and knight as well), persuaded the Roman general Varus to march out of camp and then ambushed him in wooded country. Just where the slaughter took place and whether Arminius acted treacherously or courageously (or both) are still matters of conjecture, but the Battle of the Teutoburg Forest has always been regarded as a pivotal episode in the history of Europe. Further, the story has been employed since ancient times to personify the opposition between civilization and freedom, embodied, respectively, in Roman governor and native prince.[4] As might be expected, the battle was a popular literary subject in Germany; in his play *Die Hermannsschlacht*, Heinrich von Kleist had used the incident in an unsuccessful attempt to arouse the German peoples to action in a war against Napoleon, the type of the foreign oppressor. Thus, the defeat of Varus by Arminius was traditionally interpreted typologically as representing the triumph of liberty over oppression. Morris must have had something of the same sort in mind when he wrote *The House of the Wolfings*; its relationship to northern history and German nationalism could be seen as roughly analogous to the relationship of the *Song of Roland* to European history and French nationalism. The events related in the *Song of Roland* are, of course, only verified by historical research in the loosest possible sense; its action bears almost no relationship to actual events. *The House of the Wolfings*, more closely paralleling actual events in its plot, is a vehicle for Morris's interpretations of these events for his own time.

To Morris, Rome was the archetype of tyranny, "the great curse of

[3] Henry Hatfield, in "The Myth of Nazism," in *Myth and Mythmaking*, p. 204, suggests that this incident contributed to the making of the "Nazi myth" as well. See also Joachim C. Fest, *Hitler*, trans. Richard and Clara Winston (New York, 1974), p. 389.
[4] See S. A. Cook, F. E. Adcock, and M. P. Charlesworth, eds., *The Cambridge Ancient History*, X (New York, 1966), 373 ff.

the ancient world";the defeat of one of its marauding armies by the men of the great wood is a type and symbol of the overthrow of the false by the true throughout history. The Roman soldiers and their leaders are depicted by Morris as arrogant and ruthless, waging their wars for unworthy purposes of personal ambition. (In his cupidity and personal ambition, the Roman leader of *The Wolfings* is rather like some of the leaders in the Germanic campaigns described by Plutarch in his *Life of Julius Caesar*.) Interestingly, however, the bravery and prowess of the Romans as warriors win them the respect of the Goths, who revere above all courage in warfare. By contrast, the Men of the Mark are defending their homeland and ancient way of life (which includes, incidentally, the practice of human sacrifice— the inference being that whatever is done out of sincere adherence to ancestral beliefs and customs does not constitute cruelty or brutality).[5]

Morris himself seems to shrink not at all from the most grisly details of battle; in this, *The Wolfings* is reminiscent of a number of his early Pre-Raphaelite poems and tales, such as "The Haystack in the Floods," as well as the *Iliad* and the bloodier sagas. The gore, in other words, is a traditional part of the heroic literature of which *The House of the Wolfings* is an outgrowth; not reprehensible in itself, its rightness or wrongness results from the motives of the participants. Physical characteristics are used symbolically in *The Wolfings*, as elsewhere by Morris, to denote the spiritual states of the combatants. While the Goths are physically attractive, being predominantly red-haired or blonde with blue eyes, the Romans are "swarthy," "brown-faced," and so on. The foul-favored Hunnish invaders of *The Roots of the Mountains* repeat this pattern, as do the bestial despoilers of *The Well at the World's End*. Morris is nearly always medievally conventional in thus symbolically characterizing his protagonists and antagonists.

The Goths are consistently idealized throughout *The Wolfings*. Even the combination of prose and verse, which has made the work seem difficult or even eccentric to some readers, is directed toward this idealization.[6] Morris must have come across numerous examples of

---

[5] Lemire, p. 161; for Morris's attitude toward Roman armies, see his impassioned remarks on the overthrow of Rome by the "Fury of the North," in "Art and Socialism," *Works*, XXIII, 204; on human sacrifice see *Works*, XIV, 51, for the passage telling how the daughter of the war-duke of the Markmen was "nothing loth, but went right willingly" to her sacrifice.

[6] Paul Thompson calls *House of the Wolfings* "the worst of all" the romances with its "vacuous narrative and silly rambling speeches . . . alternated with unsettling sections in verse" (*Work of William Morris*, p. 158). See also E. P. Thompson, *Romantic to Revolutionary*, pp. 677–78.

traditional narratives, sagas and chronicles as well as folktales, that employ both prose and verse. Lord Raglan, in *The Hero*, points out that it is the most important parts of such narratives that appear in verse form;[7] Morris similarly employs "rhyme and measure" for the speeches of his characters on ceremonial occasions or when they express feelings or ideas of great import. In other words, the verse represents an elevated form of communication. Further, all characters in the tale seem to be capable of framing their thoughts in verse at appropriate moments. Morris may have been trying to suggest that the democratic dignity of Germanic tribal life actually caused each individual to develop into a poet. For he believed strongly that art should be created by all members of society, thus becoming an integral part of the life of the people, not the exclusive province of an elite group isolated from the organic body of society. His ideal, expressed in his lectures on art, was "art made by the people and for the people, a joy to the maker and the user" (XXII, 80). The ability to burst into song is a symbolic by-product of the primeval freedom of tribal life.

The overthrow of the Roman invaders by the Men of the Mark, then, is a symbolic incident—a parable for modern times, denoting the timeless pattern of human events in which tyranny arises in order to be vanquished. Whether a Hegelian dialectical view of history can be read into this is another question, but it is certain that Morris means his readers to be conscious of history, and history not only extending from Roman times to the nineteenth century, but aeons stretching back into a hazy primordium. To this end Morris employs what might be described as a three-fold time level: a historical perspective characteristic of all the prose romances (and the translations and mature narrative poems as well). First, the narrator is quite frankly addressing himself directly to a Victorian audience; there is no use of the "lost manuscript" device dear to nineteenth-century writers. This contemporaneity is particularly striking in the opening pages of *The Wolfings*, where Morris compares the width of a river to the "Thames at Sheene when the flood-tide is at its highest" and the architecture of the House of the Wolfings to a "church of later days that has a nave and aisles," and explains that the Men of the Mark had an equivalent to a modern jury (XIV, 3, 6, 7).[8] Thus Morris interprets the deeds of the past for an audience of his contemporaries, fulfilling the ancient role of the bards who sang *Beowulf* or the *Iliad*. Like these ancient bards,

---

[7] Lord Raglan, pp. 239–42.

[8] Morris continued to stud the romances with contemporary geographical comparisons; for examples see *Water of the Wondrous Isles*, *Works*, XX, 193, and *Sundering Flood*, *Works*, XXI, 2, 11. His verse prologue to *The Story of the Volsungs and Niblungs* is addressed to "English Folk" who "speak the English Tongue" (*Works*, VII, 289–90).

he too remains outside the action, even effacing himself to the point of frequently reiterating such phrases as "the tale tells" and the like.

Bearing in mind this complex of time perspectives, we may better be able to appreciate Morris's reasons for using the pseudoarchaic language that he developed for these romances. It has been pointed out that the prose style of the romances grew out of Morris's earlier renderings of the sagas, in which he closely imitated Norse vocabulary and syntax; Morris was probably influenced as well by the well-known Victorian "Teutonizers" of English, E. A. Freeman, F. J. Furnivall, R. C. Trench, and William Barnes.[9] Critics have been irritated by the language of the romances; most of these objections seem to me, however, to stem from differences in taste rather than any objective criteria, for the language is neither difficult to read nor hard to understand. The truth is that the distinctive style Morris developed for his romances is not peculiar or eccentric but a sensible and original response to a literary problem. He was faced with the same difficulty all translators and writers of historical fiction must face: how to convey the essence of a civilization different from one's own in language intelligible to contemporary readers. The complexity of this problem is abundantly apparent from reading a few prefaces to modern English translations of any classic; attempts to solve it have been made in a variety of ways. Morris's solution was to invent a diction that was foreign to Victorian England yet understandable to sympathetic readers; he is obviously trying to suggest his conception of the style of Gothic language spoken by the Wolfings in an age when writing was almost unknown among them and, in consequence, no record could be kept of their language.

The Victorian reader, then, is made aware of a time perspective at the outset: he is looking back at his own ancestors of nineteen centuries ago facing a crossroads in history, and he is seeing their traditional heroic tribal ways and values triumph over the threatening Roman slave state. (It is interesting that Morris's high opinion of Germanic tribal traditions has been vindicated by some modern historians, who credit these traditions with important influences for individual freedom on the development of Western political institutions.) What is explicit in *News from Nowhere* and *A Dream of John Ball* is here only implied: nineteenth-century European man is also at a crossroads: only by heroic self-sacrifice like that of Thiodolph can he save the future.

---

[9] See Henderson, p. 109. A good discussion of the Teutonizers can be found in Austin Warren's informative article "Instress of Inscape," in *Victorian Literature: Modern Essays in Criticism*, ed. Austin Wright (New York: Oxford University Press, Galaxy Books, 1961), pp. 182–92.

But time-perspective in the prose romances is more complicated than in *News from Nowhere* and *John Ball*. Morris's Men of the Mark are conscious at all times of a heroic age in the dim reaches of their own past—so much so that this heroic past is as real to them as the present. The gods, the dwarfs, and the heroes of this legendary era are the subjects of their art work and permeate their thinking and their speech. The Goths' life of present deeds lived amid the atmosphere of the past thus effects a confluence of time. The deeds of Thiodolph and the other heroes of the Mark in successfully staving off the Romans are in reality the acting-out of an age-old pattern, and the Men of the Mark represent all mankind. Their tribal history is a paradigm of the cultural development of man, developing from a nomadic hunting society into an agricultural people, learning the use and manufacture of iron implements: "they came adown the river; on its waters on rafts, by its shores in wains or bestriding their horses or their kine, or afoot, till they had a mind to abide; and there as it fell they stayed their travel, and spread from each side of the river, and fought with the wood and its wild things, that they might make to themselves a dwelling-place on the face of the earth" (XIV, 3). Thus the reason for presenting and interpreting this historical pattern for Victorian England: this society too must rise to the challenge and renew itself by heroic dedication to the common good. Morris wrote elsewhere: "In short, history, the new sense of modern times, the great compensation for the losses of the centuries, is now teaching us worthily, and making us feel that the past is not dead, but is living in us, and will be alive in the future which we are now helping to make." To what extent *The House of the Wolfings* was inspired by Marxist ideology is a point of some disagreement, although it is tempting to see Rome as standing for the corrupt and enslaving capitalist system.[10] Even so, the tale does not require a Marxist interpretation to make its point—and this point is much the same as that of *John Ball*.

The lesson of *The Wolfings*, then, has to do with individual heroism. The experience of Thiodolph in this, his last battle, illustrates well Morris's conception of the nature of heroism. For he is one in a long line of characteristic Morrisian heroes—a line that includes most notably Sigurd, Beowulf, Bellerophon, Aeneas. Following the writing of the early Pre-Raphaelite poems and stories and up to the time of the prose romances, Morris had been reworking traditional materials—writing translations, or, more accurately, redactions, of Greek myth and legend as well as Germanic saga and epic. The selective

[10] "Preface to *Medieval Lore* by Robert Steele," in May Morris, *William Morris: Artist, Writer, Socialist*, I, 288; see Hulse, p. 103, and Thompson, *Romantic to Revolutionary*, p. 676.

manner in which he chose to treat this material is in itself revealing—and I have dealt with this subject to some extent in earlier
chapters. Now, in the late eighties, with the prose romances, Morris is
beginning to extrapolate more freely from the patterns and themes of
this traditional material. The most striking pattern, which occurs
many times throughout the works of Morris, is that of the great hero
who saves his people, always at risk of personal cost and sacrifice.
Thiodolph, of course, must give his life in the endeavor. But he has a
choice—in fact, the same choice faced by Achilles: he can become a
great hero and die gloriously, or he can repudiate his heroic destiny
and live ignominiously. In both cases the choice is possible because of
the intervention of a supernatural woman; in Achilles' case his divine
mother, Thetis, in Thiodolph's, his Valkyrie wife, Wood-Sun, who
gives him a magical, though curse-ridden, dwarf-wrought hauberk.
This hauberk has the contradictory qualities of protecting the life of
the wearer while simultaneously dazzling his senses so that he will
disgrace himself as a warrior. The hauberk is thus a fitting symbol of
the heroic dilemma—recalling the girdle worn, to his shame, by
Gawain in his encounter with the Green Knight. Morris's heroes must
choose freely to accept the personal consequences of their destinies.
But Thiodolph's choice also shares in the issues involving the wanderers of *The Earthly Paradise*. As I have argued in my earlier discussion of that poem, Morris's larger inferences are that the selfish and
regressive choice made by the wanderers in deserting their home-
lands and seeking the earthly paradise of eternal life is wrong because
it is a paradoxical denial of life, which continually demands of mankind heroic self-sacrifice. Wood-Sun holds out to Thiodolph a vision
of unending love—a paradisaical ecstasy for which he is at first
willing to sacrifice his people:

> "No ill for thee, beloved, or for me in the hauberk lies;
> No sundering grief is in it, no lonely miseries.
> But we shall abide together, and that new life I gave,
> For a long while yet henceforward we twain its joy shall have."
> [XIV, 23]

Thiodolph's internal conflict parallels the external warfare between
Roman and Goth; when he conquers the temptation of the hauberk,
the tide of battle changes and the Gothic victory is assured. It is fitting
that Thiodolph's corpse should be treated with the greatest reverence
by his people, for he has sacrificed more than they can know. Even so,
he is revered as one who will return to lead his people in a future hour
of need—this is the mark of the greatest heroes.

The hauberk's potency includes the ability to make its wearer lose consciousness of time; in this respect it is closely related to Thiodolph's love for Wood-Sun, whose love also confers oblivion to time. Thus Thiodolph, when he has fallen unconscious in the midst of battle, dreams of times past. But this is a regressive rejection of the demands of time: Thiodolph's subsequent action in giving his life for his people is in fact the renewal and fulfilling of the past—of time. Hence the importance of the well-developed historical depth of *The Wolfings*. The hero, by accepting his destiny, saves his people through his heroic sacrifice, which symbolically renews the past and brings back the lost golden age. This, as we have seen, is a pattern that is at the very basis of *The Earthly Paradise* and *Sigurd the Volsung*; Morris will continue to play upon it in subsequent romances.

It is plain, then, that in *The Wolfings* the supernatural woman, in her opposition to the heroic values of this primitive society, becomes the focus of a choice between escapism and action. Morris would always opt for action; but in subsequent romances the sacrifice would not be so complete or so tragic. After *The Wolfings* the prose tales truly become *romances*, in the sense of ending happily. But they are constructed out of the same themes and situations. This is clear in Morris's next prose romance, *The Roots of the Mountains*, which in several respects is a sequel to *The House of the Wolfings*.

With *The Roots of the Mountains*, we are once again in the region of the Italian Alps, at a somewhat later time, again deliberately left vague, but most probably around the middle of the fifth century A.D. when waves of Hunnish invaders swept through central Europe. The tribal migrations that figure importantly in the background of the story (during which the related tribes of the Wolf were separated) may have been based on those that actually took place in the late fourth century because of pressure from the east by Huns. At this time the Romans gave the Germanic tribes land between the Danube and the Balkan range, where, their tribal organization left intact, they lived under their own laws as federates of the Roman empire.

At any rate, in *The Roots* Morris shows us once more a pre-Christian Gothic people defending their homes and lives against marauding tyrants—this time, the Dusky Men, the ugly and bestial Huns. As in *The Wolfings*, their way of life is idealized in a way that reminds one of the utopian society of the future depicted in *News from Nowhere*:

Thus then lived this folk in much plenty and ease of life, though not delicately nor desiring things out of measure. They wrought with their hands and wearied themselves; and they rested from their toil and feasted and were merry: tomorrow was not a burden to them, nor yesterday a thing which they would fain forget; life shamed them not, nor did death make them afraid.
As for the Dale wherein they dwelt, it was indeed most fair and lovely, and

they deemed it the Blessing of the Earth, and they trod its flowery grass beside its rippled streams amidst its green tree-boughs proudly and joyfully with goodly bodies and merry hearts. [XV, 11]

The isolated Dale is remote from Roman civilization, the moral inferiority of which Morris suggests by referring to it in inverted Biblical language as "the Plain and its Cities" (XV, 20). (As a matter of fact, the moral superiority of the German tribes over the Romans of the fifth century was attested by Salvian; Morris at least had precedent for his judgment.)[11] Although Morris indicates so only obliquely, the tribes of the Wolf who are reunited in their common cause against the Huns are actually descendants of the Wolfings of *The House of the Wolfings*. For we learn that the tribes now known as the Woodlanders of Burgdale and the Men of Shadowy Vale came by separate ways into the mountains as they fled their ancient home "Midst the Mid-Earth's mighty Woodland of old" (XV, 288), displaced by an enormous horde of foes. The banner of the tribes of the Wolf, like that of the earlier Wolfings, carries "the image of the Wolf with red gaping jaws" (XV, 294). This Wolf is much more than merely a totem. The wolf has traditionally been a symbol of Germanic military societies and thus suggests symbolically the dedication to action that is so vital, in Morris's view, to the renewal of the world. Mircea Eliade suggests that the military associations of the wolf constitute a survival from early initiation practices among Germanic peoples, in which the donning of wolfskins plays a part. According to Eliade, the shape-changing episode in the *Volsunga Saga* when Sigmund and Sinfiotli put on wolfskins and become wolves is likewise such a survival in literary form. Now, initiation is a ritual embodying the concept of rebirth (of which we shall have more to say in the next chapter), and so the Wolf is an animal having ritual associations with the concept of renewal on individual and tribal levels. On a cosmological level, the image on the banner is an emblem of the Ragnarok when, according to Snorri's *Edda*, Fenrir's Wolf will burst his bonds and advance with huge gaping mouth, his upper jaw reaching the sky and his lower jaw on the earth. The very title of Morris's romance is a gnomic allusion to the manner in which Fenrir's Wolf was bound: again according to the *Edda*, the roots of the mountains are one of the six things out of which the fetter called Gleipnir was fashioned by the dwarfs. That these six things, including the beards of women, the breath of fish, and so on, are unheard of is adduced as proof that they were so used. We might reason that when Fenrir's Wolf shall break his fetters, these six things,

[11] The glorification of Teutonic life by Tacitus in his *Germania* is discussed by Fairchild, pp. 4–6.

no longer being required as bonds, will again be seen on earth.[12] Hence the title refers to what shall once more be experienced by man at the Ragnarok, or Apocalypse. The Wolf, peculiarly Teutonic in its symbolic connections, is a wonderfully appropriate emblem for Morris's tribes, and the reunification of the Wolfings' descendants constitutes not only a renewal of the glorious past—a rebirth and a return to origins—but is a type of the future world-renewal, when all things fragmentary come together as one and are transmuted into a new creation.

Thus the children of the Wolf, together with their kindred tribes of Gothic descent, numbering twelve tribes in all (enumerated and described in chapters 31 and 32), stand once more for mankind as a whole, much as the Israelites of the Old Testament have come in Christian theology to stand for generic man. The Armageddon-like battle of Silverburg, which is the climax of the tale, suggests the apocalyptic overturning of evil foretold in the book of Revelation, and the reign of peace and prosperity that follows is, indeed, a foretaste of the millennium, described by Isaiah: "now at last was the hour drawing nigh which they dreamed of, but had scarce dared to hope for, when the lost way should be found, and the crooked made straight, and that which had been broken should be mended" (XV, 223). (Morris consistently describes his visions of secular paradise in the Biblical imagery and phraseology which came naturally to middle-class Victorians from their cumulative experience of family prayers, church attendance with readings and responses, school chapels, and so forth. Morris was doubtless already well grounded in the King James version of the Bible when he decided as a young man to go into the church.)

For the central figure in these stirring deeds Morris created one of his most striking heroes, Face-of-God (also called Goldmane) of the House of the Face. With his golden hair and beauty of countenance, he fulfils Mallarmé's physical description of the hero in *Les Dieux Antiques* (1880): "Tous ont de beaux visages, et des boucles d'or flottant aux épaules."[13] Face-of-God's abandonment of his betrothed, The Bride, of the House of the Steer, for Sun-Beam, of the Wolfings, also conforms to Mallarmé's pattern, a pattern that includes such Morrisian heroes as Sigurd and Kiartan (of "The Lovers of Gudrun"). Throughout the tale, which, incidentally, is as devoid of supernatural

---

[12] Eliade, *Birth and Rebirth*, pp. 81–83; *Prose Edda*, pp. 87, 57. The phrase rendered here as "roots of a mountain" is in some translations given as "roots of stones." See Anderson, p. 384, for "roots of the mountains." "Roots of mountains" occurs also in Paul Henri Mallet's *Northern Antiquities*, trans. Bishop Percy (Edinburgh, 1809), II, 66n.

[13] *Oeuvres Complètes* (Paris, 1965), p. 1166.

characters and happenings as anything Morris ever wrote, Face-of-God gains stature as a living incarnation of the symbolic hero of legend and myth. Like all Morris's heroes, Face-of-God is loved by all women, his physical attraction being an outward and visible sign of his sexual potency, an essential concomitant of the life-principle of renewal represented by the hero. He is, furthermore, naturally recognized by all men as a leader, his magnetism resulting from his mystical destiny as a hero-savior. His power and perfection show forth the ultimate potentiality of all mankind, and his name suggests the true role of man in Morris's vision of the cosmos.

Face-of-God's destiny is symbolically apparent from the first. Morris introduces him to the reader as he stands alone in the afternoon sun, the gold of his hair resembling the yellow rays of the sun (XV, 12). Face-of-God, in fact, is an incarnation of the ancient symbol of his house, the House of the Face: "there in the hewn stone was set forth that same image with the rayed head that was on the outside wall, and he was smiting the dragon and slaying him; but here inside the house all this was stained in fair and lively colours, and the sun-like rays round the head of the image were of beaten gold" (XV, 15).[14] The monster against whom he will lead his people is no literal dragon but the insidious power of tyranny and oppression made manifest in a corrupt society of men—here, that of the Hunnish nomads. Face-of-God, in leading his people, a chosen people, to glorious victory, combines in his person not only their present and future but the legendary history of the Goths as well. As Folk-might, the brother of Sun-Beam, says of him: "He fared in the fight as if he had been our Father the Warrior: he is a great chieftain" (XV, 369).

Morris's early prose romances, then, are founded in a complex of millennial motifs, primarily that of a great and conclusive battle between the forces of evil and a chosen people led by a legendary hero, a battle that at once validates the past (history) and assures the future. Mircea Eliade, in *Myth and Reality*, comments on such millennial themes in terms that are illuminating to the understanding of Morris's work. The revolutionary fervor that gripped nineteenth-century Europe, beginning with the French Revolution, he points out, was marked by a widely held underlying belief that, through the process of cataclysmic revolt, a return to noble and virtuous origins was being effected. Hence the enthusiasm of that century for history (particularly in the form of national historiographies), which is, after all, a way of establishing those origins. This is the deeper significance of Morris's "Aryan" enthusiasm. Eliade writes: " 'Aryan' represented

---

[14] See also XV, 8.

at once the 'primordial' Ancestor and the noble 'hero,' the latter laden with all the virtues that still haunted those who had not managed to reconcile themselves to the ideal of the societies that emerged from the revolutions of 1789 and 1848. The 'Aryan' was the exemplary model that must be imitated in order to recover racial 'purity,' physical strength, nobility, the heroic 'ethics' of the glorious and creative 'beginnings.' "[15] The extent of Morris's Aryanism is generally unnoticed in current writings about him, probably in reaction to the ghastly consequences of these beliefs having been carried to their logical, if insane, conclusions in this century. But the fact is that nineteenth-century Aryanism was not only generated by the wider currents of the European nationalistic movements of the period but was given its intellectual impulse by the quite respectable proponents of Social Darwinism and is thus not to be merely deplored as a discredited fanaticism.

What we might call nationalistic racism not only surfaces in Morris's writings but has much to do with the types of furnishings made popular by Morris & Co. The so-called Gothic revival in architecture and furnishings had begun toward the end of the seventeenth century largely because of the need of the newly created aristocracies of Jacobean England to establish their ancestries and to legitimize or validate their position as a ruling class—in place of the saints' images found decorating genuine medieval buildings, effigies of Queen Elizabeth and other good Protestants appeared in the dwelling places of the mighty, but the style of buildings and furnishings was meant to confer upon their owners the authority of noble origins.[16] Thus one important motive behind the pre-Victorian Gothic revival was the need to establish origins, to legitimize the present by affirming a connection with the past. Morris, on the other hand, was not interested in creating, maintaining, or bolstering an aristocracy, though many of the decorating commissions undertaken by his firm served just this subtle purpose; he simply saw the Gothic style as indigenous to the common English people—hence the Morris firm popularized the humble rush-seated chairs of the rustic countryside. The rococo lines of High Victorian furniture were French inspired; such a provenance would of itself make it unacceptable to one of his Teutonic sympathies. Morris sincerely regretted that England had been deflected by the Norman conquest from what should have been

---

[15] Eliade, *Myth and Reality* (New York, 1963), p. 183.

[16] Launce Gribbin, "Gothic Revival: Revival or Survival?" Victoria and Albert Museum, London, February 5, 1974; see also Alice Chandler, *A Dream of Order: The Medieval Ideal in Nineteenth–Century English Literature* (Lincoln, Neb., 1970), pp. 186–87, on the "dynastic element" of the Gothic Revival.

its development into a "great homogeneous Teutonic people infused usefully with a mixture of Celtic blood" (XXIII, 41).[17] His opinions about racial purity and the importance of heredity might be inferred from passages in *The Roots* and *The Wood beyond the World*. Sun-Beam tells Face-of-God of the disastrous consequences of intermarriage between some tribes of the Wolf and the original inhabitants of Silverdale: "So we took their offer and became their friends; and some of our Houses wedded wives of the strangers, and gave them their women to wife. Therein they did amiss; for the blended Folk as the generations passed became softer than our blood, and many were untrusty and greedy and tyrannous, and the days of the whoredom fell upon us, and when we deemed ourselves the mightiest then were we the nearest to our fall" (XV, 111). In *The Wood beyond the World*, the Maid, playing the part of the goddess of the Bear tribe, advises the Bears upon the treatment of aliens: "ye shall make them become children of the Bears, if they be goodly enough and worthy, and they shall be my children as ye be; otherwise, if they be ill-favoured and weakling, let them live and be thralls to you, but not join with you, man to woman" (XVII, 109–10).

Morris's seeming advocacy, in these passages just quoted, of breeding humans for racial or national superiority may strike one as at variance with his political beliefs of this period, encompassing as they did the principles of *liberté, égalité, fraternité*. But the fact is that Social Darwinism was embraced by political leftists before it was seized upon by the Right as justification for its repudiation of democracy and humanitarianism. Further, as several writers have suggested, there is an intrinsic connection between National Socialism and Marxism-Leninism arising from the millennial eschatology on which both are based. Norman Cohn writes:

Beneath the pseudo-scientific terminology one can in each case recognize a phantasy of which almost every element is to be found in phantasies which were already current in medieval Europe. The final, decisive battle of the Elect (be they the "Aryan race" or the "proletariat") against the hosts of evil (be they the Jews or the "bourgeoisie"); a dispensation in which the Elect are to be most amply compensated for all their sufferings by the joys of total domination or of total community or of both together; a world purified of all evil and in which history is to find its consummation—these ancient imaginings are with us still.[18]

It is quite natural, therefore, that Morris should have immediately

[17] See also "Early England," in Lemire, pp. 158–78.
[18] Fest, pp. 55–56 (on Hitler's belief in his messianic role, see pp. 209 ff.); Cohn, p. 308 (Cohn's provocative conclusions relative to the connection between medieval revolutionary messianism and modern totalitarian movements have been considerably de-

followed *The Roots of the Mountains* with *News from Nowhere*, the socialist-inspired utopian vision which most readers have considered to be one of his finest works. For *News from Nowhere* is a prolonged description of the millennial ideal, the perfect state of society that will follow the great revolution. Straightforward as this book is, there has never been a consensus among readers and critics on how it should be taken. Philip Henderson expresses one view:

> It would be an insult to Morris's intelligence to suppose that he really believed in the possibility of such a society, where the only work that appears to be going on is a little haymaking at Kelmscott. And yet one frequently finds *News From Nowhere* seriously discussed as though it were a blue-print for a communist future. It should be obvious enough that here Morris was merely abolishing everything he disliked in the nineteenth century and replacing it by everything he nostalgically longed for. In reality it is an Arts and Crafts Utopia with very little relation to anything that we know as communism. . . . [19]

But when *News from Nowhere* is seen in relation to the prose romances, it becomes clear that it is both a blueprint for the future and a nostalgic idyll—and more besides. Further, it has everything to do with communism—it may not be a literal blueprint, but it is a poetic expression of that ideal of a noble and regenerated mankind which had impelled Morris into the socialist movement. In other words, both the writing of *News from Nowhere* and his dedication to socialism arose from his abiding faith in man's intrinsic goodness. In this idyll of the golden age, man, untrammeled by the corrupting yoke of a tyrannous class of profiteers, has found again his noble origin. It is this goal, that of the return to origins, which is the true impetus of the development of national histories and historiography. It is thus wholly fitting that Morris should envision this paradisaical state in his own England. Having begun this early phase of the romances with England's past in *A Dream of John Ball*, he ended it with a projection into England's future.

---

emphasized in the revised and expanded edition of his book published in 1970.); see also Eliade, *The Two and the One*, trans. J. M. Cohen (London, 1965), pp. 155–56, on Marxism as a millenarian eschatology.

[19] Henderson, p. 328.

Chapter VII

The Quester Triumphant: Man and Earth Made New

MORRIS'S PROSE ROMANCES are varied in type if not in style or basic theme. Following his historical romances and immediately after writing the utopian dream vision *News from Nowhere*, Morris began to evolve yet another genre, one May Morris has called *fairy romances*, a term appropriate in that it connotes elements of magic supernaturalism, which, in fact, figure prominently in *The Story of the Glittering Plain*, *The Wood beyond the World*, *The Well at the World's End*, *The Water of the Wondrous Isles*, and *The Sundering Flood*. (I have earlier suggested the term *heroic prose romance*, but this designation does not help us much to see these works in the larger perspective of literary history. Morris's romances are not like those of any other nineteenth-century romance writer with whose work I am familiar. George Macdonald's dream allegories, for instance, entirely lack the substratum of heroic tradition that underlies everything Morris wrote during his mature years. The romances of J. R. R. Tolkien come closer to Morris's than any others written since fantasy became a popular form of fiction during the pulp-magazine era. The fact that the Morrisian romance is sui generis and thus insusceptible to analysis by any generally accepted literary criteria may be a major reason for its lack of attention and appreciation among critics. Only the most intrepid readers and commentators have been willing to accept these tales on their own terms and refrain from judging them according to novelistic standards.)

But a common feature more significant than the fairy-tale provenance is the quest pattern that is basic to all these romances. With the exception of *Glittering Plain*, set in a northern tribal culture reminiscent of that in *The Wolfings*, all these later romances take place in a vaguely medieval setting recalling the romance cycles of the Middle Ages (and the world of the early Pre-Raphaelite poems). But whereas *The Wolfings* and *The Roots* are firmly grounded in the actual history and struggles of the northern races, *Glittering Plain* (1890) is clearly a fantasy. For the land in which Hallblithe stays for a year, the Land of the Glittering Plain, is the otherworld of myth and folktale, a realm of eternal youth like that sought unsuccessfully by the wanderers of *The Earthly Paradise*. The implicit authorial viewpoint, moreover, is the same as that in *The Earthly Paradise*—that is to say, the regressive searching for escape from the demands of life is at length condemned, in *The Earthly Paradise* by its own failure, in *Glittering Plain* by the example of Hallblithe's rejection. But, unlike the quest of the wanderers, Hallblithe's is not an elixir quest, for he journeys to the Acre of the Undying only to ransom his betrothed, the Hostage, and the testing he successfully undergoes requires him to reject the temptations of this erotic paradise. Hallblithe, almost Puritanical in his devotion to the ideals and traditions of his austere and moralistic tribal life, is never really tempted by the sensual pleasures available to him in the Land of the Glittering Plain and is not even momentarily attracted by the beautiful princess whose love has set in motion the abduction of the Hostage and his own beguiling. He expresses his dedication to the world of deeds and death (which is, paradoxically, the arena of life) in a stirring rebuke to his companion Sea-eagle, and this speech expresses forcefully the joy in the life of this earth that Morris himself obviously felt. It begins: "O Eagle of the Sea, thou hast thy youth again: what then wilt thou do with it? Wilt thou not weary for the moonlit main, and the washing of waves and the dashing of spray, and thy fellows all glistering with the brine?" (XIV, 256). With these images of motion, of flux, Hallblithe conveys the joy life's very transience confers on mortals.

The testing Hallblithe undergoes is not for the purpose of chastening and purifying the quester, a purpose which has come to be associated with the quest pattern since the medieval grail legends took that form. Hallblithe's character (and, insofar as we may infer it, his spiritual state) is just the same at the end as at the beginning. For him as an individual there is no real temptation, no consequent Fall, and thus no redemption. In other words, Morris is not concerned here with allegories of the human soul and its search for God—there is no Christian accommodation of the quest pattern such as we see in the grail legends or in *The Faerie Queene*.

This generalization also holds true for the other romances of this group. In each of these tales we meet heroes and heroines who from the beginning are entirely blameless, whose adventures prove and confirm their congenital worthiness. Walter, for example, in *The Wood beyond the World*, though he consorts with the malevolent Queen of the Wood, does so at the direction of the wise and virtuous Maid, so that their planned escape may not be suspected and forestalled; he is not in any sense tainted by his amorous night in the arms of the Queen and does not have to suffer, do penance, or be purified in any way. (Arthur of *The Water of the Wondrous Isles* similarly is forced to submit to a witch's lust; his subsequent suffering is occasioned not by this episode but by the necessity of forsaking his sworn lady, Atra, because of his love for Birdalone.) Ralph, Birdalone, and the other central figures of the romances are preeminently spotless in character and person for, as always in Morris, outward beauty signifies inward worth.

But what is the meaning of these last romances? Many critics would suggest, and no doubt many readers would protest, that there need be no meaning, that these are entertainments that at most represent the repressed longings of incipient old age. Morris's own continual protestations against proffered interpretations add weight to this view. And yet there is more to be said about the recurrent themes and motifs of these romances and their implications.

First, it is quite plain, as we have seen, that in these late romances, as in earlier writings, Morris is concerned with liberation from tyranny. This is basic to *The Wood beyond the World*. On the most superficial level of plot, the Maid is liberated from her bondage to the Queen; Walter, who had undertaken his wanderings as an escape from the torment of marriage to an unfaithful wife, is liberated from the more subtle slavery of an unfair social bond. It is poetically just that these two former victims should become rulers of a new kingdom—a new society—upon their escape from the Wood. Further, there is a symbolic progression in the social orders they encounter in their adventures. Upon leaving the Wood, which is presided over by a cruel and tyrannical queen, where both are humiliated and threatened because of their positions in this corrupt order, they pass through the land of the Bears, a primitive tribe of herdsmen who as yet are ignorant of agriculture. On leaving the superstitious Bears, who have accepted the Maid as their goddess, they are escorted to the beautiful city of Stark-wall by the elders who, according to tradition, are awaiting their appointed rulers to come down through the same mountain pass through which their forebears traveled to found the city.

Thus the experience of Walter and the Maid is a paradigm of the history of civilization—from oppression to a new beginning, represented by the primitive Bears, to an advanced and harmonious civilization governed in an enlightened and beneficent fashion. As king, Walter continues and refines this just government: "first he bade open the prison-doors, and feed the needy and clothe them, and make good cheer to all men, high and low, rich and unrich" (XVII, 128). Thus a millennial period of peace and harmony is instituted. It is important to note that Walter's reign of prosperity is gained through a rededication to the ancient values of courage and devotion to duty. This is made clear in the emblematic choice made by Walter immediately before the elders hail him as king. As one of the tests to be undergone, he is asked to choose between two kinds of raiment: "one was all of robes of peace, glorious and be-gemmed, unmeet for any save a great king; while the other was war-weed, seemly, well-fashioned, but little adorned; nay rather, worn and bestained with weather, and the pelting of the spear-storm" (XVII, 119). Walter rightly chooses the battle dress, symbolic of action, of deeds, rather than the peace robes, associated here with weakness, cowardice, and pride of place. (Walter's choice brings to mind a number of similar choices made by Morris's heroes: I have already compared the choice of Thiodolph in *The Wolfings* with that of the wanderers of *The Earthly Paradise*; similarly, Hallblithe of *Glittering Plain* correctly chooses the world of deeds.) This militancy of attitude is always presented as admirable in Morris's writings. Just as Walter, together with the Maid, comes to the city through the same mountain pass as their leaders of old, thus standing in their place, so his values and ideals are those of past times—and the success of the future results from an affirmation of the past.

In *The Well at the World's End* (1896), the longest and unquestionably most complex of all Morris's romances, the same issues are of paramount importance. Here the hero, Ralph, dedicates himself at the beginning to a life of deeds when he rejects his parents' desire that he remain at home and leaves to seek the greater world. The plot of this romance is intricate, but one of its main threads is the overthrowing of threatening tyrannical forces, culminating in the apocalyptic defense of Ralph's homeland, Upmeads, at the end. The psychological and spiritual significance of these imaginary events to Morris himself is underscored by the revealing remarks of May Morris to the effect that Ralph's home, the High House of Upmeads, was an extrapolation from Kelmscott Manor itself: "the King's sons start on their adventures from the very door of Kelmscott Manor transformed into the palace of a simple-living kinglet, and the second page describes closely the placing of our home between river and upland, with the ford at the corner where the harvesters in *News from Nowhere* landed at their journey's end" (XVIII, xix). Of Kelmscott Manor, Morris once wrote: "It has come to be the type of the pleasant places of earth, and of the homes of harmless, simple people not overburdened with the intricacies of life; and, as others love the race of man through their lovers or their children, so I love the Earth through that small space of it."[1] Kelmscott had come to be the center of Morris's world—a home in every sense of the word, inextricably bound up with his own life and thus a personally symbolic focus for the earth, home of mankind.

[1] Quoted in Sparling, p. 73.

Miss Morris continues in the interesting passage quoted above to point out that most of the locale of the early part of Ralph's adventures is based on the antiquity-rich downland country to the south of Kelmscott—including White Horse Hill and the Early Iron Age hill fort Uffington Castle. Morris had been fascinated by this country since his schoolboy days at Marlborough; such remnants of the remote past continued to interest him deeply all his life; and he wove them into the setting of *The Well* to enrich its time perspectives. As for Kelmscott Manor, its identification with the High House of Upmeads actually is fanciful in the extreme: Kelmscott Manor, a late sixteenth-century farmhouse, is like the medieval hall described in *The Well* only in the gray stone of its exterior, but the point is that Morris had a considerable emotional stake in this book, that he identified Ralph's home with his own, and, most importantly, that he identified Ralph's quest with his own. (Morris may have been inspired to place at Upmeads the great Armageddon-like battle that is the culmination of Ralph's heroic career by the fact that important battles had been fought in the Kelmscott area during the Wars of the Roses and the civil wars. He wrote of these battles in "Gossip about an Old House on the Upper Thames";[2] he also digresses into a description of the history of the area in the opening passages of his unfinished and still unpublished novel set in a village obviously based on Kelmscott.[3] Thus history has happily cooperated with Morris's psychic apprehensions.)

Now, the quest pattern is inextricably associated with the concept of initiation, that is, a ritual transformation of the quester into a new state of being, or rebirth. Initiation patterns proliferate in all Morris's romances; for instance, the Land of the Glittering Plain is reached twice by Hallblithe after experiences in caves, suggesting symbolic entries into the womb of Nature before rebirth. Caves figure importantly in *The Well*—Ralph buries the Lady in a cave and lives with Ursula in a cave during the winter before completing their journey to the well of life. The Lady and Ursula of *The Well* and Birdalone of *The Water of the Wondrous Isles* dress like men—here is the motif of "temporary androgynization and asexuality of novices" discussed by Mircea Eliade in *Birth and Rebirth*;[4] Ursula refuses to wear men's clothing after drinking from the well, that is, after her initiation is complete. Birdalone escapes from, and returns to, the witch's hut naked, and Walter in *The Wood beyond the World* is made to present

---

[2] May Morris, *William Morris: Artist, Writer, Socialist*, I, 364–71.
[3] British Museum Add. Ms. 45, 328.
[4] Eliade, *Birth and Rebirth*, p. 44; see also pp. 36–51 passim, and idem, *Myth and Reality*, p. 80.

his naked body for inspection by the elders of Stark-wall; we see in these episodes the ritual nakedness common to initiation rites. Such symbolic initiatory episodes are common to the heroic literature with which Morris was intimately familiar, such as Jason's passage through the Symplegades or Aeneas' experiences in caves, and, of course, their counterparts occur often in the medieval romances he knew so well.[5] Morris seems to have grasped intuitively not only the great symbolic significance of the initiation pattern (without guidance from writers on cultural anthropology) but also the tremendous imaginative appeal of such strange episodes. They lend an air of mystery to the romances, lifting them above the banality of mere adventure. Ralph's initiation is quite complex, progressing through several levels, beginning with the gift from his "gossip" Katherine of the mysterious necklace of blue and green beads and climaxing in the drinking of the water of the well of life (though Morris does not so name it). Through the intervening experiences, including his wanderings in a labyrinthine wood (like the entrails of the earth), Ralph is not really transformed, but, rather, develops naturally from a beautiful young man into a semidivine culture hero who is thereupon enabled to redeem his society—that is, to effect, in part, the rebirth of the world into new life. The real significance of the initiation symbolism is that the world is reborn as man regains his primeval perfection.[6] This is no Christian quest for a heavenly vision that is granted only to those who have risen above and renounced the world (compare the equivocal experience of Galahad in Morris's early poem "Sir Galahad: A Christmas Mystery").

Whereas the wanderers of *The Earthly Paradise* had sought the land of eternal youth in the West, associated of old with death, Ralph finds the well in the heathen East, where the dawning sun symbolizes the beginning of new life. As he starts out, at first heading south toward the warmth of life and love, he greets and blesses the world: "Now, welcome world, and be thou blessed from one end to the other, from the ocean sea to the uttermost mountains!" (XVIII, 20). This dedication to the earth is reiterated throughout the two volumes of *The Well*—when, for instance, Ralph speaks to the people of the Land of Abundance as their dead Lady would have done: "Live in peace, and love ye the works of the earth" or when, even more dramatically, he

[5] See Eliade, *Images and Symbols: Studies in Religious Symbolism*, trans. Philip Mairet (London, 1961), pp. 155 ff.; idem, *Birth and Rebirth*, pp. 64–66; and W. F. Jackson Knight, "Cumaean Gates," p. 2 of *Vergil: Epic and Anthropology* (New York, 1967), for an extended treatment of this subject.

[6] Eliade, *Birth and Rebirth*, p. 59, suggests that the concept of the rebirth of the cosmos has always been closely associated with primitive initiation rites.

drinks of the water of the well and cries out: "To the Earth, and the World of Manfolk!" (XIX, 151, 83).

Ralph's words are borne out by his deeds as, on his return, he gathers to him a conquering host, annihilates the would-be oppressors of his homeland, and institutes a preternaturally long reign of prosperity and peace (but a peace won and maintained by the might of the sword). For Ralph is a great military leader whose very aspect terrifies and paralyzes his foes as he confronts them unarmored and unhelmeted, like the humblest of the shepherd warriors in his company. Like Alexander the Great, whose footsteps Ralph retraces to the dry tree and the well, Ralph is invincible. His luck is noted and remarked upon by all who meet him in the course of his adventures; and we find, in the last chapters, that his quest, prophesied and prepared for by those who are "somewhat foreseeing," is a fulfillment of the ancient prophecies of the people of the Bear, the shepherds. In short, Ralph is the one looked-for, the renewer of the age of gold. Thus Ralph does not merely resemble Alexander in being a great leader and warrior, but, because he, like Alexander, is born to greatness, he is likewise an incarnation of the recurring heroic ideal. The Alexander romance cycle, which is obviously the major inspiration for Morris's romance, is of considerable importance in interpreting it. Alexander's life is an instance of the confluence of myth and history—the ideal and the actual. Further, for the Middle Ages as well as for later antiquity Alexander was, in the words of Elizabeth Hazelton Haight, "the prototype of all aspirants to the dominion of the world."[7] Morris means that his readers should be aware of these matters, and so insistently mentions Alexander again and again throughout *The Well.*

Ralph's great destiny is from the beginning apparent in his great beauty of form and character, for Ralph in truth has no spot or blemish. He need not be chastened or purified; he is the type of the new man; that is, he embodies the endemic perfection of mankind, which must become apparent when the unlovely fruits of selfish ambition—tyranny, cruelty, poverty—are purged and eradicated and a prelapsarian state of innocence, or nobility, is regained. As the Innocent People beyond the mountains called the Wall of the World (which they call the Wall of Strife) explain it: "Now our folk live well and hale, and without the sickness and pestilence, such as I have heard oft befall folk in other lands . . . Of strife and of war also we know naught: nor do we desire aught which we may not easily attain to. Therefore we live long, and we fear the Gods if we should strive to

[7] Haight, trans. and ed., *The Life of Alexander of Macedon by Pseudo-Callisthenes* (New York, 1955), p. 8.

live longer, lest they should bring upon us war and sickness, and overweening desire, and weariness of life" (XIX, 65–66). The Innocent People need not seek the well, for they have not fallen into corruption. In short, they represent an ideal and unfallen state of society where unnatural greed and ambition have not changed man from his primeval state of earthly happiness. Here death is welcomed as a friend, lest men grow weary of life.

The other societies Ralph encounters on his symbolic eastward journey to the well, or source of life, likewise suggest stages of civilization, growing successively more primitive as, traveling eastward back through time, he approaches the origins of life: starting out from a Christianized feudal system, he meets with despotic tyrannies in eastern cities situated among terrible mountains and desert wastes (inspired by the topography of Iceland) before reaching the Innocent People beyond the Wall of the World, and finally travels unpeopled volcanic wastes before reaching the well. The bird that lights unafraid on Ursula's shoulder in a forest region near the well signifies that Ralph and Ursula have reached symbolically a stage of harmony with nature—in short, this is a paradisaical interlude expressing itself in images traditional throughout the literature and religions of the world.[8]

On another level, which we might call psychological or spiritual in another author's work, Ralph must experience death before he finds new life. The dry tree, surrounded by the corpses of those who sought the well in vain, symbolizes this death, foreshadowed by the death of the Lady, which plunges Ralph into despair and marks the end of his boyish naiveté. (But what the Lady represents lives on in Ursula, who takes her place in the quest and in Ralph's affections.) The dry tree irresistibly suggests another level of interpretation—it was a pre-Christian symbol of death, associated paradoxically with the Tree of Life, and it is certainly used in that sense by Morris. Trees have long had symbolic associations with the cross and are used interchangeably as symbols of the crucifixion and, hence, of Christianity.[9] A dead tree suggests that Christianity is dead—or a source of death, as is Morris's tree standing in a poisonous pool. The dry tree is only a waymark on the road to the well of life—it must be passed because it is not the goal of the journey. The Fellowship of the Tree exemplifies medieval ideals of chivalry based on Christianity, but, like Christianity, they are limited. Further, Christianity is an otherworldly religion, and the cosmic tree is a traditional focal point for crossing into

[8] See Eliade, *Images and Symbols*, pp. 166–67.
[9] On the incorporation of the symbols of the cosmic tree and the center of the world into the symbolism of the cross, see Eliade, *Birth and Rebirth*, pp. 119–20.

the otherworld; but the tree is dead. There is no otherworld, and thus, no getting beyond this world. (The legend of the dry tree, like the legend-laden life of Alexander in its entirety, is a further instance of the confluence, or, in this case, confusion, of myth and actuality: it was extraordinarily popular in the thirteenth century, when it figured importantly in numerous romances, and the tree itself even appeared on maps. Supposed to have "marked the eastern extremity of the known world," it was placed in the vicinity of the Terrestrial Paradise on the thirteenth-century Hereford map by Richard de Haldingham, and many travelers claimed to have visited it.)[10]

Ralph and Ursula note that the dead seekers do not wear the talismanic beads of questers after the well; that is to say, not being among those chosen by destiny for the Fellowship of the Well, they must needs fail. One may wonder at this point whether the exclusivism of this fellowship is not more than a little undemocratic and whether it is not inconsistent for the egalitarian Morris to have posited such a situation in an idealistic work of fiction. But the hierophantic elements of *The Well* suggest the same kind of millennial thinking we have already noted in the earlier romances. The mystic Fellowship of the Well is a chosen group, much as are the barbarian Goths, or Aryans, if you will, of *The Wolfings* and *The Roots*, who are to lead the world into a glorious millennial age. These, the chosen, represent all mankind. In the story of Ralph of Upmeads, destined to become a great leader of men, Morris makes explicit what he implies elsewhere: destiny chooses its agents; all has been arranged since the beginning of time; man's role is to recognize and rise to his own destiny, no more, no less. Further, any man is chosen if he only realize that destiny. Morris spoke as follows about those fallen in the American Civil War: "many thousand men of our own kindred gave their lives on the battle-field to bring to a happy ending a mere episode in the struggle for the abolition of slavery: they are blessed and happy, for the opportunity came to them, and they seized it and did their best, and the world is the wealthier for it: and if such an opportunity is offered to us shall we thrust it from us that we may sit still in ease of body, in doubt, in disease of soul?" (XXIII, 212). This speech expresses clearly the meaning of Ralph's quest and explains why the gold cup at the well is inscribed "The Strong of Heart Shall Drink from Me" (XIX, 82), and *not* "Those Who Drink from Me Shall Be Strong of Heart." That is, all those who are strong in heart will accept their destined mission, and in the fulfillment of the quest will find what they have always been. (If this sounds disconcertingly like a comment on *The*

---

[10] See Rose Jeffries Peebles, "The Dry Tree: Symbol of Death," pp. 59–79, in *Vassar Mediaeval Studies*, ed. Christabel Forsyth Fiske (New Haven, 1923).

Wizard of Oz, let us remember that Baum also drew on the tradition of the quest.) Ralph's greatness is confirmed and brought to fruition by the struggles and hardships of the journey, but it is his own intrinsic worth which makes him into a hero-king. By contrast, we are told that the foolish King of Goldburg wasted the gifts of the well on pomp and luxury; his portion was death.

The deeper signification, then, of the Fellowship of the Well is not that it is a body of the elect. In fact, *The Well* bristles noticeably with some rather pointed egalitarian preachments by example: Ralph gives up his horse and fights unprotected so as not to have an advantage over the lowliest of his shepherd followers; though a king's son, he weds a yeoman's daughter, Ursula, whose "heart is greater than a king's or a leader of folk" (XIX, 215). Throughout the romances, as a matter of fact, Morris democratically takes his heroes and heroines from all strata of society: Walter, in *The Wood beyond the World*, is a merchant's son; Birdalone is a child of the poor; Osberne in *The Sundering Flood* refuses knighthood because it would not be consistent with his yeoman heritage.

But Ursula's parentage is of minor importance; her true relations are the other beautiful, yet doughty and militant, women who figure in Morris's writings from *Sigurd the Volsung* on, just as Ralph is cast in the mold of other Morrisian heroes. These warrior-maidens abound in *The Wolfings* and in *The Roots*: in *The Wood* it is the Maid who plans and directs the escape from the evil forest. In *The Well* Ursula, by virtue of her courage and stamina, becomes an equal partner in the quest and, rather than being conventionally rescued by the hero of romance, herself saves Ralph at the dry tree. In fact, Morris's egalitarianism is nowhere more evident than in his depiction of women as the equals of men both in spirit and in body.[11] Far from the ethereal creatures of the courtly love tradition and the Victorian stereotype (and far too, we might note, from Janey Morris's enjoyment of ill health), they were born in the pages of Germanic saga. If they are not completely liberated sexually (their maidenly virtue always being preserved until union with the hero), neither are most of their prototypes of heroic literature.

Morris indulged his fascination with these self-sufficient women by making one of them the central figure of the posthumously published *Water of the Wondrous Isles*, the last romance he was able to put into

---

[11] Richard Mathews, in *An Introductory Guide to the Utopian and Fantasy Writing of William Morris* (London: William Morris Centre, 1976), p. 16, suggests that *The Water* "presents the startling view that society can be redeemed through integration of the psyche, and . . . social and political revolution can be carried out only after effective personal liberation, women's liberation as well as men's."

finished form. In this tale Birdalone's adventures subsume a number of the various roles and situations experienced by other Morrisian heroines, most notably the Lady in *The Well*. Like the Lady, Birdalone grows to womanhood in an isolated woodland cottage as the thrall of a witch and is tutored in secret by a fairy godmother figure who prepares her for escape to the world and the life of mankind. (A similar situation occurs in *The Wood*.) In *The Sundering Flood* Elfhild's unsympathetic aunts take the place of the witch figure; Dame Anna, wise in spell-making, is her tutor and helper. (The fragment *Desiderius* contains the germ of this same situation.) Morris's repetition of this motif underlines its importance: symbolically, the interlude with the witch in an almost inaccessible forest suggests a kind of enforced separation or isolation from life itself, an isolation that must be ended by the slave herself, as it is in these cases, when she is reborn through the initiatory instruction by those wise in the lore of the earth, such as an elder or even the spirit of an ancestor. When the Lady in *The Well* and Birdalone in *The Water of the Wondrous Isles* return to these forest huts, their solitary sojourns suggest initiatory ordeals—symbolic returns to the womb (the hut) surrounded by chaos (the forest). The witch, who embodies in each case an unnatural and perverted force, must be overcome or annihilated so that her victim may not only be liberated but united with the greater life of the earth. It is symbolically fitting, therefore, that Birdalone's tutor should be an earth spirit, a faerie queene of the wood, whose name, Habundia, suggests the abundance and fertility of the earth, the antithesis of the perverted and barren sexuality of the witch, and Birdalone's true heritage. So Birdalone and Arthur are at last blessed by Habundia as very children of the earth (XX, 360).

The pattern of separation and isolation ended by union and generation is centrally important in the romances and is the deeper significance of the emphasis on sexual love so noticeable in all of them. Morris's heroes and heroines are all devastatingly attractive to the opposite sex, though occasionally this may be unconvincing to the reader. (It is difficult, for example, to reconcile Birdalone's fatally potent sex appeal with some of her Girl Scout speeches and actions.) But this sexual attraction is an outward sign of the inner generative force working through the lives of these characters, overcoming unnatural restraints and privations in order to bless the earth and bring forth the abundant fruit of love and brotherhood. Even the luxuriance of their hair suggests their kinship with the burgeoning life force of the earth. And the erotic appeal with which Morris invests the frequently bare feet of his heroines seems, at least in part, to come about through the intimacy of their physical contact with the earth.

In an earlier chapter on *The Earthly Paradise* I have discussed the significance of Venus and Diana as they appear in the tales of that work, Diana being associated with celibacy and death, Venus with sexuality and life. In the romances Diana's associations with death and sterility are attributed to the witch figures, while the hunt-maiden heroines blossom into love goddesses. (Morris frequently compares their beauty to that of goddesses of old.) In their mixture of militancy and nubility, the heroines of Morris's prose romances suggest a blending of the archetypal female roles of Aphrodite and Artemis—an emblem of this reconciliation is the reiterated description of Birdalone in her huntress garb, armed with bow and arrow.

Numerous episodes in the romances are emblematic in function. As a matter of fact, Morris remarked in an 1892 biographical talk that his poems "are rather of the nature of a series of pictures" (XXII, xxxii), and he might have included the romances in this observation. In *The Well*, for example, the rock carving called "The Fighting Man," which is an important waysign for seekers after the well, suggests the militancy and commitment to action essential for the Strong of Heart, who are to renew their lives at the well, and, further, is a natural association with the military leader Alexander the Great, an early traveler to the ends of the world, and Ralph, who follows in Alexander's path to become a Fellow of the Well and a warleader. (Morris's description of the huge rock carving in an inaccessible location above a mountain pass suggests that he may have been inspired by the highly important archaeological find called the "Record of Darius" on the rock of Behistun near Kermanshah in Persia. Deciphered at the British Museum by 1857, this inscription in three languages made possible the deciphering of cuneiform tablets and the discovery of the Gilgamesh epic, that most ancient of all accounts of the quest for immortal life. The rock of Behistun was thus, in every way, a most significant gift from the past and a most appropriate model for "The Fighting Man.")

Earlier in the plot, an arras in the Castle of Abundance, where Ralph awaits the Lady before setting out for the well, depicts the story of Alexander, foreshadowing Ralph's subsequent adventures. Similarly, in an earlier episode Ralph sees the play of Saint George killing the dragon and, shortly after, in his first encounter with the Lady, is able to effect his own rescue of a lady in distress. In *The Water of the Wondrous Isles* the magic boat in which Birdalone escapes the witch stops at several islands that have no real plot function other than to suggest emblematically the basic theme, isolation followed by union, which is the pattern of the plot. Upon leaving the enchanted Isle of Increase Unsought, where the three damsels are held captive by the sister-witch, Birdalone comes to the Isle of the Young and the Old, inhabited only by children and an old man who has no memory. Next are the Isle of the Queens, where an enchanted company of women mourn a dead king, and the complementary Isle of the Kings, where a dead woman lies in state among an enchanted throng of armed men. The last island lying between Birdalone and the Castle of the Quest, toward which she is bound, is the Isle of Nothing, a barren desert where she is trapped in an obscuring mist. The first three of these islands are emblematic representations of perverted states of society in which parts of family units exist in unnatural isolation and consequent paralysis. The last, the Isle of Nothing, suggests the sterility resulting from such perversions and the frustrations of nature. Long afterward, on Birdalone's return voyage to the witch's house by the waterside, she finds these islands somewhat returned to normality: the Isle of Nothing become populated and fruitful; the women and men of the Isle of the Queens and the Isle of the Kings aroused from their enchantment (their unsatisfied lust emphasizing their incompleteness); the old man gone from the Isle of the Young and the Old. We might infer that these changes are the result of the destruction of the Isle of Increase Unsought together with its witch-mistress. At any rate, there is evident a liberation from a debilitating or atrophic enchantment that would isolate, separate, wither, and annihilate humankind; what Birdalone sees on her way back to the forest of Evilshaw is a renewal of life not yet complete but promising that her journey will end in a lovers' meeting, as indeed it does, ending her long separation from Arthur. Renewal is foreshadowed in the magical serpent ring given Birdalone by Habundia before she escapes the witch and in the serpent shape assumed by the escaping spirit of the sending boat after her return to the witch's cottage, the serpent, who sheds his skin and renews his life, long having been a symbol of regeneration (compare the serpent in the Gilgamesh epic, who eats the life-giving plant).

The pattern of separation followed by union and restoration is graphically developed in Morris's last romance, *The Sundering Flood*, which tells the story of two lovers who grow up separated by an impassable river and of their individual quests to find each another and be united. This tale has its roots in the topography of Morris's beloved Iceland (and May Morris tells us that the central situation was inspired by a contemporary Icelandic novel [XXI, xi]). As Morris drew upon the Berkshire and Wiltshire down country dear to him for both *The Well* and *The Water*, so in his last tale he found inspiration in the land of the sagas, which had helped significantly to shape his thinking.

Morris did not have time to develop *The Sundering Flood* as he
seems to have planned,[12] but, despite the relative lack of development
toward the end, this last tale shows clearly its affinity with its predecessors. Osberne, like Ralph and Face-of-God, is created in the
mold of the archetypal hero of saga and myth, singled out from
childhood to become a glorious leader by a destiny manifesting itself
in supernatural helpers. Like Ralph, Osberne has luck, plain for all to
see in his face, and the elfin sword Boardcleaver, "fashioned by the
fathers of long ago" (XXI, 51) is in fact an attribute of his innate
prowess rather than a source of it. The mysterious Steelhead, who
initiates Osberne into manhood by the Imposition of Hands and who
gives him the magical sword, is a spirit of the earth, one of the
"warriors of while agone" (XXI, 53), and may not come into builded
towns. (Anthropologically, Osberne's initiation is a classic example of
tutelage by the spirit of a dead ancestor.)[13] Osberne is, in fact, an
incarnation of ancient heroic values reasserting themselves in a new
age in order to revitalize and restore a nation. His significance as the
agent of rebirth and renewal is emblematized in his boyhood victory
over the would-be tyrant Hardcastle, an experienced warrior. The
analogy between Osberne's challenge of the champion and David
going out to fight Goliath (perceived by the women of the household)
is significantly appropriate. The wonderful child Osberne brings
together the past and future: his youth is a promise of the future as his
manly deeds vindicate and reaffirm the values of the past.

Osberne's glorious career as the Red Lad, the bane of tyrants, does
not lead him into kingship; this, the most democratic of all Morris's
heroes, returns to his home to live out his life among his own, the free
goodmen of the uplands. Like Ralph and Birdalone, he does not
forsake his heritage but returns to his origins, healing and protecting
the land that cradled him. This is the noblest end to which heroism
may be put, and Morris's homecoming heroes and heroines complete
and make whole their lives in the circular pattern of their quests,
separation overcome and union achieved. The idea of returning to
origins is allied to the millennial eschatological themes recurrent in
Morris's writings, as we have seen in the previous chapter. Man has
been separated from his origins (earth, life, the unfallen state) and
must achieve reunification.[14] Morris's heroes come from the earth
and return to it in death, forever a part of the unending cycle of life.
Like Morris, they accept the human condition, its limitations as well
as its glories.

[12] May Morris discusses this matter in *Works*, XXI, xi–xiv.
[13] See Eliade, *Birth and Rebirth*, pp. 39–40.
[14] See Eliade, *Myth and Reality*, pp. 21–38.

The implicit "message" of the "fairy romances," then, is plain: heroism is not dead; the earth calls to each man and woman in her hour of need; she will be saved and revitalized by those of strong heart who heed the call; and those are blessed indeed who give their all to destiny. Morris once described himself as "careless of metaphysics and religion, as well as of scientific analysis, but with a deep love of the earth and the life on it, and a passion for the history of the past of mankind" (XXIII, 280). On another occasion he remarked, "In religion I am a pagan" (XXII, xxxii). That is to say, Morris's concern first and foremost was for the life of this earth, and the romances would be anomalous indeed if they did not evidence the same abiding concern for our earthly life that is so abundantly plain in everything else Morris undertook during the years of his maturity. Because the romances emphasize and mythicize the dimensions of human life, they constitute an important part of Morris's work, complementing his personal struggles in the realms of architecture and crafts, as well as politics. And this in addition to their being in themselves delightfully unique works of art.

Chapter VIII

Youthful Dreams of Doom: Morris as a Pre-Raphaelite

I HAVE ARGUED in previous chapters for the necessity of seeing Morris's lifework as a consistent whole, endeavoring to show how his writings, both prose and poetry, can be seen as integral parts of that whole. Persuasive support for such a view requires that we consider all aspects of these writings, and so we must see how his early poems are related to the patterns and themes of the later works. I have placed this essay toward the last, out of chronological sequence, not because I believe Morris's early work is either less or more important than the later (although many writers have considered it solely important), but because I believe that some new understanding may be gained by considering it within the context of all Morris's writings, and with the benefit of hindsight. We may fall into the teleological error that resulted in some late eighteenth-century writers being regarded as "preromantic," but, as a corrective to any such lack of focus, there is a respectable body of criticism treating the early poems, at least, as a discrete body of literature.

The 1858 volume does not lack unity. If we read the poems of *The Defence of Guenevere* as a body, not unduly concerning ourselves with separating them into groups according to type or provenance, we are struck with certain recurrent themes and situations. It has been usual, however, to group the poems of this volume according to provenance, whether Malory, Froissart, or "fairyland," but this sort of classification, even were it as straightforwardly simple as it at first appears, really tells us nothing in itself.[1] It is not even clear that Morris himself made such a clearcut distinction between the "historical" background found in Froissart and the legendary and even mythical material of the Arthurian cycle and related folklore; at any rate, it is more profitable to consider the unity of the poems afforded them by their thematic relationship.

The youthful poet concentrates relentlessly on the frustration of thwarted endeavor, the agony of enforced constraint and paralysis. The dramatic poem "Sir Peter Harpdon's End" is a case in point.

[1] See, for instance, Lionel Stevenson, *The Pre-Raphaelite Poets* (Chapel Hill, N.C., 1972), pp. 138 ff., and Ralph Berry, "A Defense of Guenevere," *Victorian Poetry*, 9. No. 3 (Autumn 1971), 278–79. But Berry goes beyond these classifications and points out important thematic connections.

Trapped in an indefensible castle with rotting walls, Sir Peter, a Gascon knight in the English service, awaits attack by the French knight Guesclin. After his inevitable capture, he is executed by a reluctant Guesclin in acquiescence to the malicious petitions of his cousin, Sir Lambert, whose life Sir Peter himself, unwisely merciful, had spared. The poem ends as his betrothed, Lady Alice, hearing a song about Launcelot, ruefully observes that Sir Peter was as valiant as he and yet could avail nothing but to die, and wonders if songs and stories will be made of them in years to come.

This is not a cheerful poem. Though Sir Peter's courage arouses the admiration of his sworn enemies, he must die despite their pity, and though Launcelot's heroic deeds of a legendary past are sung in the streets, that song ends with Launcelot's death:

> To his death from his birth
> He was muckle of worth,
> Lay him in the cold earth,
>   A long grave ye may delve.
>
>   [I, 61]

For it is his son Galahad, not Launcelot, who has earned glory in heaven:

> Right valiant was he
> God's body to see,
>   Though he saw it not.
>
>   [I, 61]

It is difficult to read this poem as a glorification or celebration of the Middle Ages, though such an interpretation of all Morris's early poetry is often urged. It certainly evidences Morris's profound understanding of life in the times chronicled by Froissart, but this is not to say that Morris presents that life with unreserved and uncritical approbation. "Sir Peter Harpdon's End" is actually a rather cynical poem suggesting an underlying conception of basic human frailty and helplessness beyond' the remedy of social reform based on medieval or any other models. The crumbling castle in Poitou is emblematic of a crepuscular and enervating element in human life which, already in the fourteenth century, makes it necessary to look, somewhat futilely, to the past or, alternatively, a future in heaven for salvation. In its implications and its tone, "Sir Peter Harpdon's End" is typical of its companion pieces in *The Defence of Guenevere* volume.

Except for the title poem of that volume, "The Haystack in the Floods" is perhaps the best known of all Morris's poems, and deservedly so. The bardlike objectivity of the narrator of this pathetic tale is a brilliant stroke and is responsible for the understated effectiveness of its macabre images. This effect of objectivity is analogous to that created in "Sir Peter Harpdon's End" by that poem's dramatic form, and the implications of its action are very much like those of the action in "Sir Peter." In both poems there is an inexorable process of annihilation already in motion in the opening stanzas; as Sir Peter waits hopelessly for unavoidable defeat, so, in "Haystack," Jehane and her lover, Sir Robert, ride inevitably into the waiting ambush of Godmar and his men. Jehane, sobbing "for pure doubt and dread," has a sense of foredoom that is emphasized in the question:

> Had she come all the way for this,
> To part at last without a kiss?
> Yea, had she borne the dirt and rain
> That her own eyes might see him slain
> Beside the haystack in the floods?
>
> [I, 124]

Both "Sir Peter Harpdon's End" and "The Haystack in the Floods" convey strongly the nightmare mood of frustration, the sense of man caught in an ineluctable web of circumstance, of threatened limitation, even extermination. The evocative realism of their settings contributes powerfully to their emotional impact: Sir Peter Harpdon's castle is real, yet its rottenness foreshadows the malaise expressed in the song of Launcelot's progress to the grave and Lady Alice's disillusioned remarks about human valor; the sodden haystacks amid the watery waste suggest a soured and rancid fertility corresponding to the aborted love of Jehane and Sir Robert. Realistic, too, in a modern sense of the word, is the cynical view of human nature implicit in both poems: betrayal is at the heart of the action in "Sir Peter Harpdon's End," as Sir Lambert's machinations at length overtake Sir Peter; and Jehane and Sir Robert are the victims not only of "That Judas, Godmar," but of Robert's own men, who bind him for his enemy. It is implied that Jehane is to be put to death for betraying her own people, but, as in "Sir Peter Harpdon's End," the question of national loyalties has become confused and meaningless; Sir Peter dies loyal to the English, but as Sir Lambert points out to him: "You are a traitor, being, as you are, / Born Frenchman" (I, 43). Sir Lambert's sadistic delight in taunting his cousin, who is about to be executed, is echoed in the gruesome pleasure taken by Godmar and his men in murdering Sir Robert before the eyes of Jehane. The emphasis in these poems on man's brutality, his lust, and his selfishness underscores the mood of hopelessness and despair.

But the realistic action, description, and dialogue tend to obscure

Dante Gabriel Rossetti: *The Tune of Seven Towers*. (Courtesy of The Tate Gallery, London.)

from the appreciative modern reader the fact that these poems have much in common with other somewhat less-admired poems on more fanciful subjects. "The Tune of Seven Towers," for instance, was not inspired by Froissart but by Rossetti's watercolor of the same name. This deliberately murky poem is as vaguely dreamlike as its inspiration, but nevertheless conveys unmistakably a sense of motiveless doom enveloping its characters. Interestingly, R. L. Mégroz has called the painting "ominous," and it has been pointed out by Nicolette Gray how the enclosed spaces in which Rossetti set his figures suggest a sense of airlessness and confinement.[2] The speaker of the poem, perhaps "fair Yoland of the flowers" herself, is, as a test or task, sending her lover Oliver to the haunted Seven Towers, where he will almost certainly die and thus become another of its ghosts. It is not clear why the task is necessary, and the speaker does not appear to desire Oliver's death (she is both enchantress and victim), yet it is necessary that the ritual be enacted. (One is inevitably reminded of Browning's "Childe Roland to the Dark Tower Came.") The lack of realistic motive, here consonant with the dream quality of the poem, throws into relief the pattern of doom that controls Yoland and Oliver. They are in truth acting out a nightmare of entrapment in the meshes of a malign destiny that broods over many of these early poems. This sense of entrapment or imprisonment frequently finds literal expression, for instance in the mysterious and puzzling "Spell-Bound."

"Spell-Bound" opens as the speaker mourns his enforced paralysis, echoed in the stasis of the surrounding countryside with the fields of corn waiting in vain for the reaper. As he compares the "golden land" to a forsaken bride, his metaphor grows more and more particularized until we realize that he is envisaging his own deserted and despairing bride. Speaking of his dreams of love now lost in the past, the speaker laments:

> But when . . .
> . . . in these arms I folded thee,
> Who ever thought those days could die?
>
> [I, 105]

Thus his lost love and the dead past have now somehow become the same thing, and we see the symbolic significance of the speaker's enchantment: he is isolated and imprisoned in a nightmarish present, bound "round with silken chains / I could not break" by the "wizard whom I fear" (I, 106), that is, by time, whose chains inevita-

---

[2] Mégroz, *Dante Gabriel Rossetti: Painter Poet of Heaven in Earth* (1929; rpt. New York, 1971), p. 245; Gray, *Rossetti, Dante, and Ourselves* (London, 1947), p. 20.

bly imprison all humanity, separating them from all that they love and from what gives them life. "Spell-Bound" is not, strictly speaking, a dramatic monologue; it is, rather, a complex blend of interior monologue, third-person narrative, and dramatic monologue, and the speaker, like the enchanted Prince in "Rapunzel," is effectually imprisoned in his own consciousness as well as in a capsulated present. But, as in the dramatic poem "Rapunzel," the immediacy of first-person narration in "Spell-Bound" emphasizes the theme of discontinuity between past and present. "Spell-Bound" can, in fact, be read as a poem about the paradoxical nature of time; it passes too quickly, separating us from the "happy days of old," and yet it also passes too slowly, as we feel the isolation and unhappiness of the present: "How weary is it none can tell, / How dismally the days go by!" (I, 104).

On a literal level "Spell-Bound" remains obscure. We do not know why the speaker has been set "Above the golden-waving plains" or exactly what is happening in the last two stanzas, when the speaker seems to be addressing his beloved, now come to him with his "good sword." The speaker may be a ghost, a disembodied consciousness bound geographically to the vicinity of a churchyard grave; this reading would explain why he hears the "tinkling of the bell" and sees the "cross against the sky." The last stanza ("But I shall die unless you stand,/ . . . Within my arms") then must be interpreted to mean that the spirit of the speaker will fade unless nourished by the companionship of his beloved, who is perhaps to join him in death by committing suicide with his sword. (The *Liebestod* motif is important in several other poems of this volume, as we shall see.) Morris was quite capable of writing lucid poetry, as other poems in this volume and later works attest. We must assume, then, that the murkiness of this and some others of these early poems was deliberate; Morris at this point was simply not primarily interested in the rational exposition of plot. By submerging the facts of the action, he emphasizes the immediate feelings of his speakers and makes us share their anxieties and frustrations as we try to fathom the meaning of their experiences. In the deliberateness of his poetic obfuscation, Morris actually transcends the famous (or notorious) obscurity of Browning, to whose poetry *The Defence of Guenevere* owes so much: it is not at all clear that Browning intended to befuddle his readers; Browning's poems rarely leave us totally in the dark as to what has actually happened, although we may wonder at some length about the meaning of what has happened.

Another somewhat equivocal poem, "The Little Tower," similarly turns upon the theme of imprisonment, a theme central to the poem no matter how it is read. It is not clear whether the speaker, Isabeau, and his retinue are on their way to the Little Tower, a stronghold in the fens, in order to rescue his lady, who is imprisoned there, or to imprison themselves voluntarily in order to withstand a siege by the king. The fenland setting, the defiance of the king, and the intimation of witchcraft all suggest that this poem may have been inspired by the historical episode when Hereward the Wake held out against William I on the then island of Ely (Hereward's exploits, actual and legendary, were given currency during the 1840s by Thomas Wright and others.).[3] At any rate, the speaker's courage and self-confidence are unmistakable; he is a man of action, not given to introspection or to dreams of the past. He looks instead to the future, even beyond his own death, when the visible evidence of his deeds will survive him:

> The Little Tower will stand well here
>
> Many a year when we are dead,
> And over it our green and red,
> Barred with the Lady's golden head.
>
> [I, 101]

Thus in "The Little Tower" the entrapment motif appears as an externalized symbol and only becomes meaningful as a symbol when the poem is seen in relation to the entire *Defence of Guenevere* volume. To some extent this is true of several other poems that center upon rescue from prison.

"A Good Knight in Prison" is the story in dramatic form of the rescue by Launcelot of a Christian knight, Sir Guy, from a pagan castle where he is held prisoner by King Guilbert. Sir Guy's reunion with the Lady Mary is a renewal of the past after a surrealistically morbid interlude in the bad air of the marshland castle where the "sickly flowers" are "pale and wan" (I, 83). Here the great Launcelot fulfils the role of the life-giving hero, redeeming and renewing life. His rescue of Guenevere at the end of "The Defence of Guenevere" reiterates the pattern, though this poem deals with only part of their story, and its real point is the insight given into the workings of Guenevere's mind. The action of Morris's dramatic poem "Rapunzel," based upon the familiar folktale, also rehearses the pattern of imprisonment and rescue. (Morris invites us to remember the story of Guenevere by having Rapunzel resume her real name, Guendolen, as

---

[3] Hereward the Wake is the central character of Charles Macfarlane's two-volume novel *The Camp of Refuge* (1844). Wright's "Adventures of Hereward the Saxon" may be found in his *Essays on Subjects Connected with the Literature, Popular Superstitions, and History of England in the Middle Ages* (1846; rpt. New York, 1969), II, 91–120.

soon as, the witch's enchantment broken, she has been rescued from her imprisoning tower.) At the heart of these traditional tales lies the same folklore motif that is the basis of that other legend so fascinating to Rossetti and his circle, that of Saint George's rescue of the Princess Sabra, the subject of several Rossetti watercolors and a series of stained glass panels designed by him, as well as the Morris paintings on the famous "Saint George" cabinet and the later designs and gouache by Burne-Jones.

But, of course, rescue is not usually part of the pattern in the generally pessimistic *Defence of Guenevere* poems. "In Prison," placed importantly at the end of the volume, urges a sense of despairing isolation, together with guilt and doom, effects emphasized by the falling rhythms of the verse:

> all alone,
> Watching the loophole's spark,
> Lie I, with life all dark,
> Feet tether'd, hands fettr'd
> Fast to the stone. . . .
>
> [I, 145]

Here the speaker's situation suggests that of a fetus imprisoned in the womb, yearning to be born, anticipating the initiation symbolism of the later prose romances and recalling the rite de passage of the Prince in "Rapunzel," who dreams of waking into a new life:

> Not born as yet, but going to be born,
>   No naked baby as I was at first,
> But an armèd knight, whom fire, hate and scorn
>   Could turn from nothing. . . .
>
> [I, 65]

There is, however, no rebirth within the poem "In Prison." And even more pessimistic is another of the "prison" group, the forthrightly affecting "Riding Together," in which the speaker recounts how he and his friend, together with their "little Christian band," were bested in battle by their pagan foes and then made to ride one last time together as he was taken prisoner and bound to his friend's corpse. Now he looks forward only to joining his friend in death:

> We ride no more, no more together;
>   My prison-bars are thick and strong,
> I take no heed of any weather,
>   The sweet Saints grant I live not long.
>
> [I, 136]

"Riding Together" makes us think of analogues from heroic poetry

William Morris: "Saint George" cabinet, detail. (Crown Copyright. Victoria
& Albert Museum.)

Sir Edward Burne-Jones: *Saint George and Dragon.* (Courtesy of the William Morris Gallery, Walthamstow.)

where friendship between comrades at arms is the most exalted human relationship: the love of Achilles for Patroclus and of Oliver for Roland. But Morris's emphasis is not on the triumph of the human spirit implicit in the *Iliad* and the *Song of Roland*; "Riding Together" instead conveys a sense of desolation and hopelessness.

A sense of imminent death lurks as well behind several of Morris's dramatic monologues in which the speakers are old men remembering the past. Two of these invite comparisons with Browning's use of this form in the restraint and suggestiveness with which Morris employs it. The opening stanzas of "Concerning Geffray Teste Noire" are, superficially, a racy account by the elderly John of Newcastle of an unsuccessful attempt undertaken while in his prime to ambush a notorious Gascon thief, the Blackhead of the title. Froissart, he thinks, may be interested in the tale, he tells Alleyne, his listener: "Perchance then you can tell him what I show" (I, 81). Morris is here being historically accurate: Froissart did depend upon oral testimony, whether collected by him in his travels or relayed to him through messengers. But the chronicler would not have benefited greatly from John of Newcastle's recollections of Geffray Teste Noire, for his memories in fact center on his chance discovery, while on this campaign to entrap Geffray, of two skeletons, those of a knight and his lady who had been waylaid and murdered many years before. At length John of Newcastle's tale of adventure is transmuted into a hymn of love to the dead lady, whose "small white bones" his imagination has clothed with living flesh. The poem ends as John of Newcastle, having recollected himself to the present, tells abruptly of the inconclusive end of the ambush, of Blackhead's subsequent peaceful death in bed, and of his own reverent burial of the knight's and lady's bones beneath effigies wrought by an artisan now dead like them. The last three words of the poem, "I am old," underscore masterfully the implications of the speaker's story. His love for the lady, dead so many years, is in fact an emotionally specific expression of a yearning for all that is lost forever, for the past itself.

"Geffray Teste Noire" is a poem Browningesque in the very best sense of the word, that is, in the subtlety with which the poet causes the speaker to reveal himself without designing to do so. But while Browning's famous poems about the Renaissance and the Middle Ages evoke a sense of the past, Browning's primary interest is always in the eccentricities of character. His best poems not only reveal the often grotesque quiddities of these characters but make us realize that these individuals reflect wider truths. The Duke of Ferrara, in his combination of egoism, cruelty, and connoisseurship, capsulates the Italy of the sixteenth century. The Duke is, of course, a masterpiece of literary characterization, and, since Browning's own poetry does not consistently come up to the mark of "My Last Duchess," we should hardly expect a young poet of even Morris's precocity to approach in his first volume the depth of psychological penetration typical of Browning at his best. (But in fact the very simplicity, the one-sidedness, of many of Morris's *Defence of Guenevere* characters may in itself suggest the world of the Middle Ages and early Renaissance, a world not given to excessive introspection.) Even so, the equivocal motives and convoluted reasoning of characters like the psychotic speaker in "The Wind" or even Guenevere defending herself show that Morris was capable of following Browning's example not only in form (dramatic) and style (abrupt and jarring) but also on the deeper level of psychological insight. For our interest in "The Defence of Guenevere" is in the character of the speaker, as her incoherent argument progresses through its specious "proofs" of her innocence, in themselves a kind of exemplary catalogue of the fallacies of relevance.

The real conceptual difference between Morris's portrayal of Guenevere and any of Browning's great characterizations lies in the greater objectivity of the younger poet: Morris consistently refuses to judge his characters, while Browning cannot suspend his moral judgments even while taking the greatest delight in the delineation of villains (though individual poems most subtly avoid overt moralizing). Morris would in subsequent years abandon this kind of dispassionate perusal of humankind in favor of a symbolic simplification of character (in the prose romances, for instance, we are allowed no opportunities for equivocation in judgment). The young Morris's interest in character, coupled with this moral objectivity, looks forward to the humanitarianism of his mature years, but these poems exhibit his interest in human experience for its own sake; he had not yet begun to conceive of literature as the embodiment of ideas or human aspirations.

Another "very old" speaker, Sir John of "Old Love," recalls his own youth vividly in his memories of his lady, now the wife of the Lord Duke, when her beauty was fresh and their love hot, but he is most of all aware of what time has done:

> Her lips are drier now she is
> A great duke's wife these many years;
> They will not shudder with a kiss
> As once they did, being moist with tears.

> [I, 88]

In comparison with the destruction of love and youth, embodied in the duchess's beauty, the fall of Constantinople is a little thing:

> "these things are small;
> This is not small, that things outwear
> I thought were made for ever. . . ."
>
> [I, 87]

Anticipating the authorial viewpoint later to be developed in *The Earthly Paradise*, Morris has Sir John suspect that mere dreams of the past are somehow inimical to "true life":

> "Ah! sometimes like an idle dream
>   That hinders true life overmuch,
> Sometimes like a lost heaven, these seem. . . ."
>
> [I, 89]

The heroes of the prose romances will instinctively restore their lost heavens through action, not dreams.

"Old Love," like "Geffray Teste Noire," is remarkable for the skill and delicacy with which the poet handles the speaker's attitude toward his subject, but despite the similarities between these two poems, their excellences are not in the least redundant: part of the pleasure in reading "Geffray Teste Noire" comes from the gradual realization by the reader that the speaker's real subject is something quite different from that announced; in "Old Love" the speaker's detached weariness creates an ironic displacement: both the young man he had been and the beautiful girl he had loved are now no longer, and so he views both these vanished characters of memory dispassionately as though they were strangers. They are, in fact, inhabitants of the lost past from which his present self is forever estranged.

"Old Love" and "Concerning Geffray Teste Noire," then, treat in expository fashion what is conveyed symbolically in the "prison" or "entrapment" poems. There is expressed clearly in these poems a sense of anxiety, of frustration, of impending catastrophe, corresponding to the emotional significance of actual dreams of entrapment or confinement. Some psychologists tell us that these dreams result from memories of the birth trauma; the reiterated prison image clearly suggests the womb symbolism that writers on anthropology and comparative religion have found in initiation rites in many cultures throughout the world (discussed in the preceding chapter). Thus, on a deep symbolic level these early poems seem to arise from an awareness, fundamental if perhaps not wholly conscious, of the pattern of catastrophe and renewal underlying reality—in short, from a rudimentary millennial ontology that was to bear continuing fruit as it developed throughout Morris's life.

Inherent in millennial eschatologies is the idea that catastrophe, or the death of the old, must precede the birth of the new: in fact, the destructive process is an inherent part of the larger creative one. This is true for civilizations as for individuals, but the youthful Morris who wrote these poems had not yet addressed himself to the larger implications of the pattern in which "life must destroy life, in the unfolding of creation," as D. H. Lawrence was to express it in *St. Mawr*.[4] Morris's early poems are conceived in terms of individuals, their living and dying. Given Morris's later development, it is entirely to be expected that there should be a prominent death-wish theme in these early poems, and this theme frequently occurs in conjunction with variants of the *Liebestod* motif. This is quite clear in "The Blue Closet," which, like "The Tune of Seven Towers," was inspired by an identically titled watercolor by Rossetti. A poetic drama in form, it tells the somewhat confusing (and perhaps confused as well) story of the four ladies of Rossetti's painting, Alice the Queen, Louise the Queen, and their "Two damozels wearing purple and green." Although at least one commentator on the painting has suggested that Christina Rossetti was the model for one of the ladies,[5] others have suggested that Elizabeth Siddal, Rossetti's favorite model of this period and later his wife, modeled for all four of the ladies, who seem to have similar, if not identical, features. Rossetti was fascinated with the idea of the doppelgänger, as is evident in his drawing "How They Met Themselves," so it is quite possible that the four ladies of his watercolor are meant to suggest a mysterious quadrupling of individual identity. At any rate, both painting and poem become more interesting if the ladies are seen as identical. In Morris's poem they are imprisoned in a snowbound tower by the sea (a setting that is entirely his interpolation, since it is not indicated in the painting), allowed to sing one song once a year on Christmas Eve. They sing, remembering the past and Arthur, the dead lover of Louise: "How long ago was it, how long ago, / He came to this tower with hands full of snow?" (I, 112). As they sing, the dead Arthur returns to take his collective four-fold bride with him back to "the happy time": "For their song ceased, and they were dead" (I, 113). The identification of death with the consummation of love is foretold in the symbolically sexual episode of Arthur's sprinkling snow upon Louise's naked shoulders:

> "Kneel down, O love Louise, kneel down!" he said,
> And sprinkled the dusty snow over my head.
>
> He watch'd the snow melting, it ran through my hair,
> Ran over my shoulders, white shoulders and bare.
>
> [I, 112]

[4] Lawrence, *St. Mawr, Together with The Princess* (London, 1925), p. 85.
[5] Mégroz, p. 245.

Dante Gabriel Rossetti: *The Blue Closet*. (Courtesy of The Tate Gallery, London.)

Dante Gabriel Rossetti: "How They Met Themselves." (Courtesy of the Fitzwilliam Museum, Cambridge.)

The literal equation of death and sexual ecstasy is a recurrent motif among the Pre-Raphaelites (evident, for instance, in the "rapt" expression of Elizabeth Siddal as Beatrice in Rossetti's *Beata Beatrix* and as Ophelia in Millais's painting), but the wider implications of Morris's poem belong to him alone.

Here, then, is the whole pattern: the imprisoned ladies (or, perhaps, the one lady of four aspects) await a death that is also a rebirth into new life back in "the happy time"—that is, a renewal of the past. That this death is truly a passage to new life is hinted in the symbols of generation in the surroundings: the tower is both a phallus and a womb wherein the four women in one (the number four, perhaps, suggesting completeness) await their rebirth; it is beside the sea, apprehended by poets throughout history as a literal and figurative womb of life. The time of year, Christmas Eve, suggests further the theme of regeneration, not only by virtue of its Christian context, but because, even more basically, the Christmas celebration is a survival of the ancient equinoctial celebrations that mark the passing of the earth into a new cycle as it dies into winter and revives into spring. Arthur, then, is simultaneously a corpse, a spirit from the underworld, a demon lover, and a fertility figure, embodying within himself the intimate and mystical connection between death and the renewal of life. His name must make us think of Tennyson's two Arthurs just as the "great bell overhead . . . pealing for the dead" on Christmas Eve must bring to mind the recurring Christmas bells of *In Memoriam* and the "clear church-bells" of Christmas morn in the last lines of "The Epic" in "Morte d'Arthur." Indeed, Morris's poem can be read as a bridge between Rossetti's painting, so arresting and so profoundly meaningless (in the sense of being devoid of conceptual content), and Tennyson's richly connotative poems dealing with the death of King Arthur and his own grief for the dead Arthur Hallam.

The theme of regeneration is implicit and overt in "Morte d'Arthur": if we fail to recognize the significance of the dying Arthur's own words, "The old order changeth, yielding place to new," we must realize, with the last lines of "The Epic," that Arthur's death, like Christ's, is intrinsically connected with the rebirth of the world into new life, as the speaker's dreams of the millennium fade into the reality of Christmas bells:

> all the people cried,
> "Arthur is come again: he cannot die."
> Then those that stood upon the hills behind
> Repeated—"Come again, and thrice as fair;"
> And, further inland, voices echoed—"Come
> With all good things, and war shall be no more."

Dante Gabriel Rossetti: *Beata Beatrix*. (Courtesy of The Tate Gallery, London.)

Sir John Everett Millais: *Ophelia*. (Courtesy of The Tate Gallery, London.)

> At this a hundred bells began to peal,
> That with the sound I woke, and heard indeed
> The clear church-bells ring in the Christmas-morn.[6]

Tennyson wrote "Morte d'Arthur" during his first shock of grief at Hallam's death, and he was later to write explicitly of Hallam in terms that make clear the connection in his mind between the two Arthurs. Section 103 of *In Memoriam* is clearly an extrapolation from "Morte d'Arthur": the poet dreams of dwelling with maidens within a hall ringing with music and containing the veiled statue of Hallam. In obedience to a "summons from the sea," they board a "little shallop" and begin their journey to "eternity" (Tennyson's gloss for "sea"), all the while gathering "strength and grace / And presence" and waxing "in every limb" until they meet Hallam, "the man we loved" but "thrice as large," on the deck of a "great ship" which then bears them all together to their mystical destination, much as Arthur's funeral barge conveys him and the three queens to Avalon. Section 104, immediately following, marks the third Christmas after Hallam's death and is famous for its onomatopoeic rendering of the sound of bells. Aside from the obvious generative symbolism of ship and water, there is a noticeable phallicism in the growth or waxing of the dreamer and his maiden companions, and this becomes most obvious in the transformation of the "statue veil'd" into the "thrice as large" figure of Hallam on the ship. (King Arthur, "come again," was "thrice as fair.") Whether Tennyson himself was aware of the subliminal effects of his poem must remain a moot question, but the symbolism seems not to have been lost upon Morris, who transmutes Tennyson's images into frankly erotic terms, making his Arthur the lover of Louise. The seaside setting of Morris's poem is intrinsically related to its meaning: as the "sea-salt oozes through / The chinks of the tiles of the Closet Blue," the drowned Arthur, his hair "stiff with frozen rime" and his "eyes . . . full of sand," is on his way to consummate his love and bring death to the ladies of the Blue Closet.

This gruesome description recalls *In Memoriam*, where Tennyson, addressing the ship bearing Hallam's body to England, envisages his friend gulfed "fathom-deep in brine," his hands tossed "with tangle and with shells."[7] It is not necessary to argue that Morris had Tennyson's poetry consciously in mind when writing "The Blue Closet"; that there is some kind of associative connection among these poems seems clear. Morris seems to have perceived the underlying mythic basis of Tennyson's passages dealing with dead men and ships and

---

[6] Tennyson, "Morte d'Arthur," ll. 240, 295–303.
[7] Tennyson, *In Memoriam*, Sect. 10, ll. 18, 20.

then conceived this mythic basis or structure in analogous but entirely original poetic terms arising from his own subconscious fund of images. "The Blue Closet" is far more than a pastiche from various sources; it is a compelling symbolic poem in its own right and transcends all of its sources, pictorial or poetic.

A similar connection between eroticism and death underlies the strange dramatic monologue "The Wind," which, like many of these early poems, revolves around the central conception of isolation, or imprisonment, in the present. Here, corresponding to the paralysis of the bewitched speaker of "Spell-Bound" is the old man's unnatural immobility as he sits in his chair afraid to move and remembering the summer day on which he found his sweetheart grotesquely and inexplicably stabbed to death beneath the sheaves of daffodils he had heaped upon her bosom. This disturbing poem invites close analysis but remains elusive. The speaker's story elliptically describes a scene of violent sexuality:

> I held to her long bare arms, but she shudder'd away from me,
> While the flush went out of her face as her head fell back on a tree,
> And a spasm caught her mouth, fearful for me to see;
>
> . . . . .
>
> I kiss'd her hard by the ear, and she kiss'd me on the brow,
> And then lay down on the grass, where the mark on the moss is now,
> And spread her arms out wide while I went down below.
>
> . . . . .
>
> And then I walk'd for a space to and fro on the side of the hill. . . .
> [I, 108–9]

As in "Spell-Bound," "The Little Tower," and "The Judgment of God," the reader cannot be sure exactly what has happened in this poem. If the phrase "I went down below" is interpreted on a subliminal sexual level, we might infer that when the speaker finds Margaret dead with "blood on the very quiet breast," she has either stabbed herself in despair at having lost her honor or has been murdered by her ravisher, the narrator. In either case, the stabbing is not only a consequence of the sex act; it symbolically echoes it. Thus the act of love, as the quintessential affirmation of life, is transposed into an equivalent act of death—the stabbing. The yellow daffodils with which Margaret is covered (she is "flowered" as well as "deflowered") suggest simultaneously death (as floral offerings to the dead) and rebirth (the symbolic significance of such offerings).

One is reminded of the symbolic complexity of the flowers in *Hamlet*: the flowers Ophelia picks in her madness are an index to that madness, which causes her death, and also prefigure her own funeral offerings by Gertrude, who remarks that Ophelia's "bride bed" and not her grave should have been strewn with flowers; thus, though her lover's actions should have culminated in bringing Ophelia to her bridal bed, they have instead brought her to her grave, and her whole history is compressed into one metaphor. Reminiscent of *Hamlet*, too, is the unbalanced mental state of the speaker in "The Wind," obvious in the opening stanzas as he explains why he cannot move:

> If I move my chair it will scream, and the orange will roll out far,
> And the faint yellow juice ooze out like blood from a wizard's jar;
> And the dogs will howl for those who went last month to the war.
>
> [I, 107]

Thus, because we know the speaker to be somewhat abnormal, we are not really surprised at the incoherence of his recollections, and the puzzling elements of his story are consonant with his characterization. This speaker is one of several in *The Defence of Guenevere* who are nameless; the emphasis is thus centered on the shocking and disturbing aspects of his vivid memories.

The last stanza supplies some historical perspective, however, and a possible explanation for his tragic relationship with Margaret. Describing the ghosts of dead knights which appear to him, the speaker says:

> I knew them by the arms that I was used to paint
> Upon their long thin shields; but the colours were all grown faint,
> And faint upon their banner was Olaf, king and saint.
>
> [I, 110]

"Olaf, king and saint" is Olaf II, ruler of Norway from 1016 to 1028, who was responsible for the social reorganization of his country. Olaf allied himself with the yeomen and succeeded in breaking the power of the existing aristocratic class of petty kings. Morris's deranged speaker, who painted arms upon the "long thin shields" of the dead knights, would have been an artisan and thus of a lower class than Margaret, who walked holding a "painted book in her hand," surely an indication of wealth and leisure. During this period of intense class struggle there would have been no way for these lovers to come together lawfully; the speaker of the poem, like Browning's speaker in "Porphyria's Lover," may have murdered his sweetheart rather than lose her to another man of her own class, and the intense stress of making his decision and carrying it out may have precipitated his madness. But this we cannot know for sure, since Morris's speaker is not interested in communicating facts; he is instead absorbed in his private apprehensions of past and present, locked forever in his own consciousness. What is conveyed to the reader by this poem is the atmosphere of crazed horror and isolation, in which even an external natural force like the wind becomes an aspect of the speaker's mental search for the lost innocence of the past:

> Wind, wind! thou art sad, art thou kind?
> Wind, wind, unhappy! thou art blind,
> Yet still thou wanderest the lily-seed to find.

This refrain, though technically identical, as it does not alter throughout the poem, is also incremental, acquiring new meaning with each repetition. Beyond this, it is also a symbolic refrain which has been defined by Sister Alacoque Power as generating "another level of meaning, related to, but distinct from that conveyed in the stanza."[8] In the beginning stanzas of the poem, the wind is simply a noise disturbing to the speaker. As we learn something of his history, however, we begin to see that the ever-searching wind is a metaphor for the speaker's memory, forever wandering, forever seeking an impossible unity of purity and passion. Finally, we realize that the wind, like Shelley's west wind, is literally a destroyer and preserver in its own right, an intrinsic part of the natural process of death and rebirth. For the wind will find the lily seed, but the speaker's restless and unsatisfied mind will die with him. The speaker is thus isolated even from the cycles of nature.

Parallel in many ways to the death of Margaret in "The Wind" is the ambiguous death, in "Golden Wings," of Jehane du Castel Beau, who seemingly slays herself with a sword that is mysteriously broken. The poem opens with what Yeats has called the "best description of happiness in the world," an idyllic word picture of an "ancient castle" standing "Midways of a walled garden / In the happy poplar land" (I, 116).[9] It is a mysteriously peaceful refuge, where war and sorrow are unknown:

> no drop of blood,
>
> Drawn from men's bodies by sword-blows,
> Came ever there, or any tear.
>
> [I, 117]

This Edenic castle is a place for lovers only, and Jehane's fruitless waiting for her knight, Golden Wings, makes her an anomaly. But her suicide on the shore "Where the water meets the land" is not an act of

---

[8] *The Refrain in Nineteenth Century English Poetry* (Washington, D.C.: Catholic Univ. of America Press, 1960), p. 13.
[9] Yeats, p. 60.

despair, but of affirmation, done where the mingling elements sym-
bolize the consummation of love in the meeting of opposites: "And I
have hope. He could not come, / But I can go to him" (I, 122). Her act
brings death to this miniature world, for her death is taken by her
companions as a murder, and they go out to "meet the war." The last
stanzas tell of a world lapsed into ruin and decay:

> The apples now grow green and sour
> Upon the mouldering castle-wall,
> Before they ripen there they fall. . . .
>
> [I, 123]

The apples which fall unripened, like the broken sword, suggest the
abortive sexuality typical of *The Defence of Guenevere* poems, consonant with the motif of imprisonment and enforced stasis. But
Jehane's death has only brought into being what was inherently a
part of this world from the beginning, symbolized by the parti-
colored raiment of the dames and knights, red for life and white for
death: "Half of scarlet, half of white / Their raiment was" (I, 117).
Thus Jehane's act is a simultaneous death and consummation of
love—a catalyst for the completion of the pattern of life and death
within the world of the castle. Regardless of the blight brought upon
this world by Jehane's suicide, it is clear within the context of the
poem that this suicide is a positive action. We think of Keats's "On
Death" ("Can death be sleep, when life is but a dream?") as we see
Jehane transfigured in the morning sun, which changes "her white
feet to glowing gold," like the angel's feet in Rossetti's painting *Ecce
Ancilla Domini* (also known as *The Annunciation*).[10]

Nowhere is Morris's fascination with the paradoxical relationship
of death to life more evident than in the overtly simple dramatic
monologue "The Gilliflower of Gold," in which the recurring image of
the blood-stained yellow flowers symbolizes the ironic juxtaposition
of opposites. The speaker tells of his triumph in the day's tourney,
during which he had worn a golden gilliflower in his helmet as his
lady's token. As he murderously hews down his opponents, all for the
love of a lady, he visualizes the gilliflower, a symbol of love and life,
refreshed with their blood as if by dew, and he is inspired to victory by
thoughts of his lady's head "Bow'd to the gilliflower bed, / The yellow
flowers stain'd with red" (I, 91). Several species have been known by
the name "gilliflower," but none, I believe, has yellow and red flowers; in fact, the speaker's vision is a chromatic fantasy of love and
death: he sees his lady, who should embody his aspirations toward
love and life, in conjunction with the bloody flowers, which represent

[10] John Keats, "On Death," l. 1.

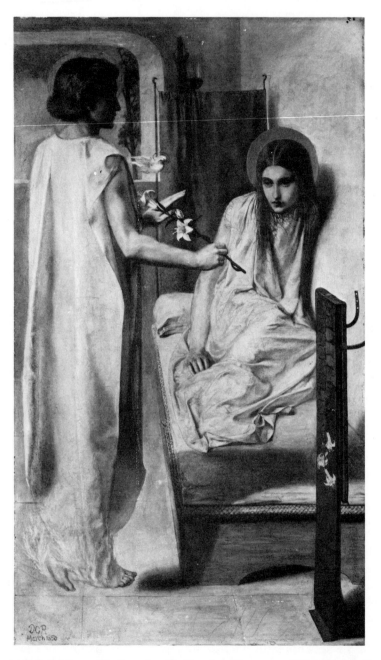

Dante Gabriel Rossetti: *Ecce Ancilla Domini.* (Courtesy of The Tate Gallery, London.)

his triumphs in a mock, yet deadly, warfare. The joyous innocence of the refrain, one of Morris's most masterful symbolic ones, provides the ultimate irony of the poem: it is at once a battle cry, a "fierce tune," and a celebration of the beauty of the speaker's lady, as the gilliflower itself is simultaneously simply a flower, the lady's favor worn by the knight, and the lady herself. (The complex relationship of the refrain to the entire poem in "The Gilliflower of Gold" is rather like that in "Two Red Roses across the Moon," which has been briefly but clearly analyzed by Sister Alacoque Power.) [11]

"The Eve of Crecy," identical in form to "The Gilliflower of Gold," is reminiscent of it in a number of ways, though rather more subtle. Both poems are dramatic monologues spoken by young men who seek glory, honor, and love by the sword. Here the speaker, Sir Lambert du Bois, while preparing for battle, thinks of his beloved, Margaret, and reflects on his poverty, but then looks to the future when his fortunes will improve and he can wed her. The irony is that the occasion for which he prepares, and on which he anticipates prancing his horse before Philip of France, is to be a gigantic debacle for the French, and Sir Lambert, in all likelihood, is to be one of the more than four thousand French knights reputed to have been killed at Crecy. The poem is thus deceptive in its overt simplicity, and its real meaning turns on the paradox by which death and dishonor come through what should have insured life by bringing fame, riches, and love.

Whereas it is quite possible to understand the fundamental meaning of "The Wind" without knowing anything of Olaf II's reign, we must know the outcome of the battle of Crecy in order to see the point of "The Eve of Crecy." Because modern readers know little of medieval history, the poem must now be annotated when it appears in anthologies of verse, but to Morris, who was so intimately familiar with all aspects of life in the Middle Ages, it must surely have seemed an obvious point that any intelligent reader would grasp. It was as natural to him to refer to an important medieval battle as it would be to a twentieth-century poet to allude to Dunkirk. The point is that Morris's poems do not have historical background; they are not poems written about particular periods or episodes. They are poems about human beings who happen to be living in the Middle Ages; they could only have been written as the result of what amounts to a mental and imaginative time-journey. Browning's poems about the Renaissance, like "Fra Lippo Lippi," or "Andrea del Sarto," which are frequently studded with arcane references to contemporary person-

[11] Power, pp. 14–15.

ages and events, give the impression of being deliberately constructed as reflections of epochs that will give the reader a short
course in art or history as he strives to understand the allusions.
Morris's poems, on the other hand, have an artlessness, a naiveté,
quite unlike anything in Browning. A closer analogue to Morris's way
of writing about the Middle Ages is the more common practice of
extrapolating from mythology, or, to be specific, Homer, as seen in
such poems by Tennyson as "Oenone," or "The Lotos-Eaters," which
require that we know the fate of Troy and the story of Ulysses.

   A third poem that groups itself with "The Gilliflower of Gold" and
"The Eve of Crecy" is "The Judgment of God." It too is a dramatic
monologue in four-line stanzas, spoken by a young man going into
battle, but this speaker, Lord Roger, struggles with a moral problem—a situation rare in Morris's poetry. Lord Roger is about to
undergo trial by combat for a wrong done in the past, probably an
ambush and murder planned by his family or clan, although the
circumstances are far from clear. (The poem has been interpreted
somewhat differently by Walter E. Houghton and G. Robert
Stange.)[12] His father has given him crafty advice on how to fight the
champion, Sir Oliver, who he fears will best him in a straightforward
combat. Thus, facing the danger of death, the speaker, like the speakers in "The Gilliflower of Gold" and "The Eve of Crecy," thinks of his
beloved, in this case, Ellayne, whom he has rescued from the stake;
because of their love, he does not fear "death or anything." Finally,
however, he instructs his man to bring others to his aid at the end of
the fight because, even should he win, he fears the hatred of the
assembled company. Lord Roger is certainly a scoundrel; yet because
we see that even scoundrels can love and fight for their lives, we do
not condemn his lack of honor. In fact, because we see that the
Hainault knights are no better, we are brought to conclude that
questions of honor and justice are truly irrelevant in this situation.
The title refers to the medieval belief that God's justice would prevail
in such trials by combat. But the speaker, though certain of his guilt
("We did that wrong"), is yet not certain of defeat by Sir Oliver. The
only reference to God in the poem is in the speaker's father's battle
advice, surely blasphemous as both father and son know themselves
to be guilty:

> "Swerve to the left, son Roger," he said,
>   "When you catch his eyes through the helmet-slit,
> Swerve to the left, then out at his head,
>   And the Lord God give you joy of it!"

[I, 96]

---

[12]*Victorian Poetry and Poetics*, 2d ed. (New York, 1968), p. 622, *nn.* 18–19.

Lord Roger is certainly entrapped and threatened with annihilation; whether he is to escape is an open question. The fact of Lord Roger's morally false position, together with the singular circumstance of having rescued his beloved from burning at the stake, must bring to mind the story of Launcelot and Guenevere. Perhaps "The Judgment of God" may be regarded as a thematic echo of the well-known poems of this volume which center on the Arthurian legends and which by their prominence dominate the whole.

Of all the characters who appear in *The Defence of Guenevere*, Launcelot is closest to the type of the great hero about whom Morris would write again and again in future years. But in "The Defence of Guenevere" and "King Arthur's Tomb" the emphasis is on Launcelot the lover, his passion and his anguish. In "King Arthur's Tomb" Launcelot's memories of past joys with Guenevere dominate the first part of the poem and, even while Guenevere berates him and herself with their sin, the reader is struck not with the ugliness of sin, of adultery and betrayal, but with the tenacity of their love, which is not even yet quenched. The bell Launcelot hears upon his lone waking could be a harbinger of his own coming heavenly salvation (foretold in "Sir Galahad") but seems almost an ironic touch, so far is he from overcoming this too earthly love.

Similarly, Guenevere's memories of past love dominate "The Defence of Guenevere"—neither she nor her creator, Morris, is concerned overmuch with her sin. Morris presents Launcelot and Guenevere as two persons enmeshed in the toils of a morality that is foreign to their natures and thus impossible for the reader to accept as other than a punishment and a yoke. The great questions of public morality and national direction that Tennyson was to weave into his monumental version of the Arthurian legends do not yet concern the young Morris, who was nevertheless later to take them up in quite a different manner. In short, these poems, so often regarded as examples of Morris's medievalism, are medieval only in their force and vitality, and are not medieval at all in their underlying philosophy — they express a commitment to the earthly life of deeds and human love that is not consonant with the prevailing otherworldliness of medieval thought as it has come down to us in actual writings of the period. And yet their overriding pessimism makes them quite different from the lusty animalism of Chaucer's more frivolous works.

Even the pure Galahad, as Morris depicts him, must struggle with earthly longings. In "A Christmas Mystery" emphasis is placed on the gulf between the beatific vision granted to Galahad, the purest of knights, and the hellish fates that befall the other seekers of the grail and their company. But the greatest part of Galahad's monologue is given to a description of the earthly longings that have troubled him throughout his vigil. Half asleep, he dreams of human love, denied him, "poor chaste body" who rides alone. Pater, writing of Morris's Arthurian poems, noted that "What is characteristic in them is the strange suggestion of a deliberate choice between Christ and a rival lover," by which he means pagan sensuousness as opposed to Christian asceticism.[13] But Galahad makes no deliberate choice; he is "musing half asleep" over memories of a pair of lovers seen kissing in a garden when Christ appears to him in a vision and argues him back into the straight and narrow path. Galahad is altogether too passive a character to inspire us with his example of spiritual choice. In short, the effect of this poetic drama is equivocal and is not made less so by its companion poem, "The Chapel in Lyoness." As Sir Ozana dies, Galahad, who has kept vigil by his deathbed in the chapel, envisions Ozana reunited with his lady in an afterlife in which the flesh is still paramount:

> Her cheek is laid to thine;
> No long time hence, also I see
> Thy wasted fingers twine
>
> Within the tresses of her hair. . . .
>
> [I, 34]

Galahad's preoccupation with the worldly deeds of Launcelot, his father, also suggests his attraction earthward. Indeed, if one brings to bear the Christian teaching that a man's thoughts are as important as his deeds, it is difficult to understand why Galahad should have deserved his vision of the grail, for these two poems convey forcefully the temptation rather than the renunciation of the world.

The medieval (or Catholic) conception of man as naturally wicked and of the earth as a vale of sorrow was never a view sympathetic to Morris, who was, in his mature years, to envision mankind's natural goodness revitalizing a beautiful earth, and though Morris was at this time only a few years past his youthful intention to go into the church, there is little indeed in his writings to suggest that he was concerned with the subject of personal salvation. It is actually rather ironic that the cliché about Morris that is still given widest circulation is that he was at once an interpreter and champion of the Middle Ages, for, though he was indisputably an authority on many aspects of that period, his turn of mind was never medieval, but something at once older and more modern: he was a pagan and a Rousseauvian roman-

---

[13] Walter Pater, "Aesthetic Poetry," in *William Morris: The Critical Heritage*, ed. Peter Faulkner (London, 1973), p. 80.

tic, a lover of the earth and of mankind, whose innate goodness was the infallible sign of his birthright—of his kinship, of his identity, with the natural world.

This is not to say that there are not many elements of the Christian tradition that find expression or, at least, parallel in Morris's work. The millennial eschatology lying at the heart of Morris's apprehension of reality (which I have earlier discussed at some length) is basic to Christianity. But the point is that this eschatology is not confined to Christianity—is, in fact, a pervading mode of thought in many religions and ancient mythologies. Morris may well have assimilated this fundamental way of seeing the meaning of history from church teachings in his youth, but it was when he encountered this same ontology underlying Marxist philosophy that he projected his true religion onto the socialist movement, with its dedication to this earth, this mortal life.

It was in fact Rossetti who characteristically thought in medieval terms, though for him Christian mysticism was more an aesthetic tool than a religion to be practiced. As everyone knows, the gold bar of heaven warmed by the bosom of the blessed damozel illustrates how comfortably Rossetti could write of earthly passions in heavenly imagery and of heavenly images in fleshly terms. "The Blessed Damozel" may be overdiscussed and overpraised, and his painting of the same name may indeed look like a Victorian church window, as one critic has suggested,[14] but together the poem and the painting do illustrate that quality in Rossetti's work that is sometimes called mystic—the synthesis of flesh and spirit in a manner that is seemingly naive but actually requires an educated way of perceiving the real world, that is, the world of sense perception. This mysticism is not really transcendentalism, a belief in the immanence of divinity working through the natural world, or world of flesh; it is rather an identification of flesh and spirit. It is more typically Catholic than Protestant, and more typically medieval than romantic. One thinks of the well-known medieval French tale "Conte del Tumbeor Nostre Dame," which tells of the tumbler turned monk performing his acrobatics, his sole method of service, for the delight of the Virgin Mary. The author who can conceive of the Virgin's image looking on this performance and the Virgin herself appearing visibly (to others) to tend and fan her exhausted entertainer and worshiper is not far in mental set from the one who can conceive of the warm-blooded damozel in heaven weeping for the loss of her lover, though the one be

---

[14]Oswald Doughty, ed., Introduction, *Dante Gabriel Rossetti: Poems* (1957; rpt. London, 1961), p. xi.

Dante Gabriel Rossetti: *The Blessed Damozel*. (Courtesy of the Fogg Art Museum, Harvard University Bequest—Grenville L. Winthrop.)

a thirteenth-century monk and the other a rebellious Victorian artist. Morris himself was to express the difference between this medievalism and his own religious sense in *News from Nowhere*, as old Hammond explains to Guest how the religious life of the new England resembles and yet differs from that of the Middle Ages:

More akin to our way of looking at life was the spirit of the Middle Ages, to whom heaven and the life of the next world was such a reality, that it became to them a part of the life upon the earth; which accordingly they loved and adorned, in spite of the ascetic doctrines of their formal creed, which bade them contemn it.

But that also, with its assured belief in heaven and hell as two countries in which to live, has gone, and now we do, both in word and in deed, believe in the continuous life of the world of men. . . . [XVI, 132]

The truth is that there was a fundamental difference between the basic world views of Morris and Rossetti at this particular period during the 1850s, when Morris was still under the influence of Rossetti's personal magnetism and artistic ideals. There can be no question that Rossetti profoundly influenced Morris, but Morris had already decided against the church and for architecture before meeting Rossetti, and he was not to continue long in the Rossetti-directed effort to become a painter. Morris returned to the sphere of the applied arts and never lost his interest in architecture.

What, then, makes Morris's early poems "Pre-Raphaelite"? For one thing, it is the historical period in which they are set. But Morris had been interested in the Middle Ages since childhood, and though Rossetti's predilection for Pre-Raphaelite subjects naturally constituted a bond of interest between the two men, Morris might have written most of his poems even had he not known Rossetti. An affinity more profound is the "aesthetic" quality apparent in the work of both men during the fifties, that is to say, the absence of an underlying moral viewpoint. Morris's objectively conceived vignettes of medieval life correspond philosophically to the particularity and inwardness of Rossetti's drawings and paintings, which Nicolette Gray has described as follows: "His pictures present a fragment of life, he has concentrated on presenting the reality of the image he saw with the greatest possible intensity, the most vivid images at moments of most complete awareness, isolated, everything directed inwards, the space confined, colour opaque, picture surface crowded."[15] This perceptive comment is as applicable to Morris's poems as it is to Rossetti's paintings. Neither man was at this period primarily interested in ideas or facts, but in feelings and moods. And it is feeling and mood

[15] Gray, p. 29.

that are communicated by Morris's Pre-Raphaelite poems. We cannot know why the color gold, for instance, recurs with such insistency in these poems, yet we are aware that Morris's private color symbols contribute something indefinable to the atmosphere of his world. Because ideology has been removed from the context of the poems, we are reduced to "interpretation" on the basis of inference, but what has taken place is an intellectual reduction and not an emotional one.

The young poet Morris was the beneficiary of the literary and artistic influences that surrounded him. The dramatic monologues of Browning and Tennyson, the Arthurian revival sparked by Tennyson, the artistic revolution given momentum by Rossetti—all these contributed something to Morris's poetry, which is yet undeniably original and even pioneering to a striking degree. I do not believe that any other Victorian writer so clearly perceived and demonstrated (very quietly) the relationship between literature, myth, folklore, and history. Consider what he accomplished in the superficially simple dramatic poem "Rapunzel."

First, Morris's choice of the most self-consciously artificial literary form, poetic drama, at once places this humble folktale in a context so extraordinary that it must be seen in an unwontedly significant light. Second, the intricate metrical patterns within this poetic drama give the tale an artistic symmetry independent of its plot and emphasize its literary quality. The use of an incremental refrain in any poetic drama is somewhat unusual; in "Rapunzel" Morris surpasses his use of this device in the other poems of *The Defence of Guenevere*. The refrain of the first and last parts of the poem is constituted by the witch's reiterated instructions to Rapunzel to let down her hair. This primary refrain occurs first after the Prince's introductory four-line stanza, then following each pair of speeches by Rapunzel and the Prince, each of which speeches is in the form of a four-line stanza and yet forms part of the speakers' independent interior monologues. The speeches of Rapunzel and the Prince have separate rhyme schemes, Rapunzel's always ending with a reference to her golden hair, and thus the last lines of Rapunzel's speeches form a counterpointed secondary refrain reinforcing the imprecations of the witch. Following a brilliant variety of soliloquies, songs, and dialogues arranged in complementary metrical patterns and during which the Prince breaks the spell of the witch and rescues Rapunzel, Morris repeats his opening metrical pattern with the final scene in the palace of the Prince, now King Sebald. The refrain is still the "harsh voice" of the witch, now in hell, and, in its final form, it expresses the essential mythic core of the tale:

> Woe! that any man could dare
> To climb up the yellow stair,
> Glorious Guendolen's golden hair.
>
> [I, 74]

Now we see at last that the simple folktale contains within it the core of the greatest myth of western man, the story of Prometheus. We think also of the Biblical story of Jacob's ladder, of the pattern of the quest and the rebirth of the quester, as Sebald, breaking his enchantment, is born into manhood through his overthrow of the witch's dark tyranny, and we see further that all this was implicit in the poem from the very beginning, where we meet Sebald the Prince "in the wood," like Dante, who begins his symbolic journey in the chaos of a dark forest.

Folktales are timeless, and the archetypal figures of prince, maiden, and witch, belong to no epoch. Morris does suggest a vaguely medieval setting with his mentions of knights and of "Norse torches"; the interpolated account by Rapunzel of the two knights who came and "fought with swords below" brings to mind Malory's account of the two brothers Balan and Balin, but also suggests the blithely anachronistic "Knight's Tale" of Chaucer, in which Palamon and Arcite are simultaneously aristocrats of ancient Greece and medieval knights as they fight for their lady Emelye. "Rapunzel" can thus be seen rather in the light of an iconoclastic mystery play, an enactment of myth consonant in setting with the other poems of the volume, and not only related thematically to them but synthesizing their themes and motifs and extending their meanings at the same time. It is truly a remarkable poem in a volume of remarkable poetry.

Conclusion

A Pagan Prophet

WRITERS ON MORRIS seem inevitably to quote in some context his famous remark "If a chap can't compose an epic poem while he's weaving tapestry . . . he had better shut up, he'll never do any good at all." This essay is no exception. But though it is much overquoted, it is a revealing statement, for Morris did not write his poetry in the belief that he was creating immortal artifacts of divine inspiration. "That talk of inspiration is sheer nonsense, I may tell you that flat . . . there is no such thing: it is a mere matter of craftsmanship."[1] Whereas the unquestionably great poets—Dante, Milton, Wordsworth, and Yeats, for instance—seem themselves to have been aware of their high place in literature before the world conceded it to them, the realistic and practical Morris seems to have realized, with no false humility, his own minority in the hierarchy. In nothing was he an innovator; his genius was not in creating new things or in expressing human truths in original imagery. Instead, he was a great adapter, one who could see the patterns inherent in all things, in the foliage and birdlife he transmuted into designs, in the great historical events of the past that he projected into the future. The typefaces he designed are derivative; the furniture made by the company was adapted from traditional designs. Tapestries, stained glass windows, epic poetry—all were traditional forms to be adapted, reinterpreted, and, if possible, revitalized. Morris was primarily a synthesizer, yet a synthesizer of genius, for what he brought together gained new integrity and force under his hands. Even if Morris had been a greater poet, it is by no means certain that his total impact upon the evolution of our civilization would have been greater. His regenerating influence has been a catalyst in many fields and, even now, his writings are attracting a new interest.

Morris's facility was extraordinary. May Morris, writing of the swiftness with which her father worked, quotes from a letter written in 1868: "To-day I took first piece of copy to printer. Yesterday I wrote thirty-three stanzas of Pygmalion. If you want my company (usually considered of no use to anybody but the owner) please say so. I believe I shall get on so fast with my work that I shall be able to idle" (III,

[1] Mackail, I, 186.

xxii). Morris wrote much of his poetry during the night, probably to occupy his restless mind while his household slept.[2] All his life he seems to have regarded his writing as a relaxing diversion from his other varied and demanding activities. In the sense that it may have been an escape for him, it may be regarded as "escapist" literature. But it was not so much an escape for Morris as a working-out of an approach to life that he himself put into practice. Embodying as they do the thoughts of a man so committed to action, Morris's poems and tales would be anomalous indeed if they advocated simply the ignoring of problems. Yet this is the interpretation they have been given by a number of critics. That Morris in refusing to claim for his work the authority of divine revelation did not argue for its implicit message has probably contributed to a pervasive misunderstanding. But if Morris failed to act as interpreter for his own books, they speak for themselves. His writings do present a point of view, however vaguely and tentatively it may be realized in any given excerpt. This Weltanschauung may be summarized in a rather crude and simplistic manner as follows: History is cyclical, and we are undergoing the decline of the civilization of the north, an inevitable process that is a repetition of similar declines in previous civilizations or world epochs; individual man, in obedience to the inexorable workings of destiny, must accept his preordained role in the cosmic ritual, whether heroic or mundane, assimilating his life insofar as possible to the world of nature, eschewing Prometheanism and accepting the simple sensuous pleasures of his short mortal life without seeking to prolong them past the appointed end of individual human happiness.

On the face of it this may seem an elaborate way to state what Morris himself expressed more simply when he remarked, "In Religion I am a pagan."[3] The cyclical ontology that lies at the root of his philosophy is not the least of the pagan characteristics of his thinking—Mircea Eliade distinguishes between Christian and pagan religions in terms of concepts of continuous, as opposed to cyclical, time.[4] But there are many kinds of paganism, and we need a more precise qualification. We might begin by noting that Morris's earth-religion, like that of the Romantics before him, is what Eliade calls a "cosmic" religion, that is, one in which natural objects are venerated as manifestations of the sacred: in religions of the cosmic type, which include "the overwhelming majority of religions known to history, . . . the religious life consists exactly in exalting the solidarity of man with life and nature." Thus the objections of Marx and Feuerbach to

[2] Henderson, p. 87.
[3] Recorded by Sidney Cockerell. See *Works*, XXII, xxxii.
[4] *The Myth of the Eternal Return*, p. 161.

religion on the ground that it "estranges man from the earth, prevents him from becoming completely human," are not valid except for later forms of religion, like Judeo-Christianity, in which "other-worldness" plays an important role.[5] In actuality, then, the existence of a Morrisian religion does not of itself necessarily imply a lack of Marxist orthodoxy on his part.

Though Morris's outlook was consistently primitivistic, his particular form of paganism is highly civilized, far indeed from a truly primitive way of thinking. Edwin A. Burtt in *Man Seeks the Divine* enumerates four basic characteristics of "civilized faiths" as opposed to primitive religion, and these are as pertinent to the Morrisian philosophy as they are to the great world religions Burtt goes on to discuss. The first is the acceptance of the principle of "universal moral responsibility." Whereas primitive man is conscious of moral obligation only toward his own group, in "the higher civilized religions this situation is left behind. A universal moral order is envisaged, and a realization of moral obligation toward all men, simply because they are men, is born."[6] Morris's efforts toward social reform place him clearly on the side of the "civilized religions," but even if this were not so, his writings continually reflect a concern for all mankind that transcends the insular interests of social or racial identifications. The Aryan fever of the nineteenth century profoundly influenced Morris, as we have seen, but when his northern poems and tales are read with attention to symbolic implications, we can also see that as his hero-figures become emblems for all mankind, so his Germanic tribes become prototypes for the community of man. Further, Morris's alternation between classical and northern subjects in *The Earthly Paradise* as well as the change from the Greek world of *Jason* to the Scandinavian world of *Sigurd* illustrates an interest in the analogies between different civilizations. It is no coincidence that Morris should have "translated" (that is, composed redactions of) the major epics of four European civilizations: the *Odyssey*, the *Aeneid*, the *Volsunga Saga*, and *Beowulf*.

Burtt's second distinction between primitive and civilized religious thought is the difference in concept about the nature of the universe itself. While primitive man's "implied cosmology is pluralistic," the civilized religions "exhibit a vigorous trend toward monism in their picture of God and of the world"; "their commitment to a universal and impartial moral order naturally leads to the notion that the universe itself is a coherent system, embracing all events and

---

[5] Eliade, *The Quest: History and Meaning in Religion* (Chicago, 1969), p. 64 *n.* 7.
[6] *Man Seeks the Divine: A Study in the History and Comparison of Religions*, 2d. ed. (New York, 1964), pp. 98, 99, 100.

rendering them intelligible in terms of uniform law."[7] The sense of inexorable destiny that pervades *The Earthly Paradise, Jason,* and *Sigurd,* is basically monistic, however much may be made of individual gods and goddesses; the supernatural spirits of the last romances have become agents of that monistic destiny.

Burtt's third point of differentiation is the "material or quasi-material" concept of the human soul common to primitive thought as opposed to the more spiritual notion of the soul's nature found in civilized religions. To civilized man the human soul is the "capacity to grow toward the realization of a universal moral ideal, and to exemplify it with responsibility and understanding."[8] Morris's most important message is that man must acquiesce in the cosmic plan —in other words, the individual must assimilate himself in thought and action to a plan which, however impersonal, is divine. It is through this capitulation of the individual will that harmony is realized on earth.

The last differentiation made by Burtt concerns man's search for happiness. To the primitive "there is nothing else in life to be seriously desired beyond the fulfillment of those cravings whose satisfaction is necessary if the conditions of physical existence and well-being are to be maintained from year to year and from generation to generation." But civilized man "commits himself to a more aspiring quest"; he is aware that "true happiness for man . . . consists rather in a transformation of these desires" so that he may "find an integrated joy in devotion to the ideal." This is the "meaning of the religious emphasis on 'conversion' . . . the 'new birth.' "[9] With regard to Morris, this last point is the most interesting of all. Chapter 3 of this study, which deals with *The Earthly Paradise,* is concerned partly with the opposition of Venus and Diana representing, respectively, the principles of generation and asceticism. Superficially, it would appear that Morris is urging unrestrained licentiousness; however, it must be recalled that the wanderers' search for a regressive state of sensual gratification results in alienation from the fruitful world in which their aged years are spent and that the singer's quest to be reunited with his beloved is frustrated as he struggles to accept emotionally what he has realized intellectually—that the past cannot live again. Just as the hero must accept the role fate assigns him, the singer, like all men, must accept the conditions of mortal existence and learn that mere human happiness (symbolically apprehended as sexual love), no matter how precious, cannot be prolonged past its appointed time.

[7] Ibid., pp. 102, 98, 102.
[8] Ibid., p. 104.
[9] Ibid., pp. 110, 108, 109–10.

In the mature romances, as we have noted in chapter 7, sexual love becomes a metaphor for the unity of man within himself, with humanity as a whole, and with the earth itself.

What is ironic about Morris's paganism is that it does not differ in practical application from the Christianity more or less subscribed to by such "establishment" poets as Tennyson and Browning. Morris was too civilized, in the best sense of the word, to become truly primitive, despite his contempt for the civilization he saw around him.

If, for the "idle singer" of *The Earthly Paradise*, we may read "Morris, the man" (and I believe it is obvious that we may), it can be inferred that Morris worked out in his narrative poems a personal philosophy that is echoed in the activities of his life. If we did not know of his explosive temper and the outbursts of frustration that have been so amply documented in the published biographical material, we might assume that he was by nature a model of effortless tranquillity and calm resignation. But the stormy and restless personality that emerges from the biographies tells us that Morris, however stoically he was finally able to face his unsatisfactory marital relationship and to deal with the social inequities and idiocies he saw on all sides, must have had to learn the hard way, like the wanderers and the idle singer, to reconcile himself to his own fate. Further, Morris's pioneering activities in the arts and in the socialist movement evince a quality of leadership that can, without sarcastic intent, be called heroic. Morris's compulsively hectic career demonstrates that he felt to some degree the call of destiny. His conception of himself as leading and educating both the leisured classes, by showing them what constituted tasteful decoration, and the working classes, by lecturing to them on art, aside from his active participation in political marches sometimes resulting in violent confrontations, suggests a latter-day culture hero educating and leading his people to a closer approximation of an ideal society, or golden age.

Morris, then, presents his view of the nature of the world in the symbolical poetic narratives and prose romances, and this Weltanschauung is apprehended ultimately in terms of personal experience. Further, lying just under the surface of the entire narration there is a tacit exhortation to the reader that he must similarly examine his personal apprehension of the world so that he may view human experience in this new way. What is implicit in the poetry becomes explicit in Morris's writings and lectures on art and socialism. These are overtly directed to the molding of new attitudes on the part of the hearing and reading audiences. In these respects Morris fits the description of the "Victorian sage" described by John Holloway in his study of Carlyle, Disraeli, Eliot, Newman, Arnold, and Hardy. One point Holloway makes about these "sages" is that in each case their various "Life-Philosophies" must be gathered, not from any one discursive statement, but from the complete body of their work (the "intersubjective" approach of J. Hillis Miller). This, too, is true of Morris. It is very difficult, if not impossible, to get a sense of Morris's distinctive way of thinking from reading just one tale of *The Earthly Paradise*, for instance. And Holloway's observation that the prophetic insights of the sage come about, not through logic, but through mystical apprehension, is equally applicable to Morris. The fact that Morris's ideas do not actually make much sense has been demonstrated clearly in Graham Hough's *The Last Romantics*, and it is unnecessary to repeat the exercise here. But it is also a fact that the truth of myth has nothing to do with logic (as Hough finally points out in his discussion of *News from Nowhere*), and Morris's works should be seen as poetic revelations of mythic truth rather than strictly rational analyses. Yeats said as much in his essay "The Happiest of the Poets":

I am certain that he understood thoroughly, as all artists understand a little, that the important things, the things we must believe in or perish, are beyond argument. We can no more reason about them than can the pigeon, come but lately from the egg, about the hawk whose shadow makes it cower among the grass. His vision is true because it is poetical, because we are a little happier when we are looking at it; and he knew as Shelley knew, by an act of faith, that the economists should take their measurements not from life as it is, but from the vision of men like him, from the vision of the world made perfect that is buried under all minds.[10]

Morris was in fact no advocate of a rational approach. In one of his lectures on pattern designing, "Making the Best of It" (1879), he describes the effect a pattern ideally should have in terms equally applicable to the design of his narratives:

At the same time in all patterns which are meant to fill the eye and satisfy the mind, there should be a certain mystery. We should not be able to read the whole thing at once, nor desire to do so, nor be impelled by that desire to go on tracing line after line to find out how the pattern is made, and I think that the obvious presence of a geometrical order, if it be, as it should be, beautiful, tends towards this end, and prevents our feeling restless over a pattern. [XXII, 109]

Morris's anti-intellectualism is abundantly evident throughout his writings (particularly so in *News from Nowhere*), and figures impor-

[10] Holloway, *The Victorian Sage: Studies in Argument* (London, 1962), pp. 1–20 passim; Miller, p. vii; Hough, pp. 95–112; Yeats, p. 63.

tantly in several tales of *The Earthly Paradise*. The scholar who deciphers the message of the riddling statue in "The Writing on the Image" and Bharam of "The Man Who Never Laughed Again," who twice uses a key, first to unlock the gate leading to paradise and second to gain the forbidden room (a quintessential paradise within a paradise), recall the clever Oedipus, whose solving of riddles eventually leads to his downfall, and the learned Faustus, whose attempt to know the secrets of the universe ends in annihilation. In Morris's view destiny is to be obeyed, not understood.

Of Holloway's sages, Hardy is the closest to Morris in point of view. In both authors there is the same emphasis on the mysteries of destiny (Hardy's famous coincidences), the same exhortation to man to assimilate himself to the processes of nature (Clym Yeobright's tragedy has quite a lot to do with the fact that in his face "could be dimly seen the typical countenance of the future," that is, it showed the modern preoccupation with "mental concern," which had replaced the "zest for existence" of earlier civilizations). Again and again in Hardy's books, the Promethean characters (which include almost all of his protagonists) are chastised by the cruel twists of fate, "life's little ironies," for which his books are so well known. The great difference between Hardy and Morris is, of course, that while Hardy's novels are just as symbolic in their way as Morris's poems and romances, Hardy uses a realistic technique, at least on the surface, whereas Morris's writing is much closer to what Northrop Frye calls the "mythical mode."[11] As Frye so incisively points out, literary design that approaches the extreme of myth (as opposed to naturalism at the other extreme) "tends toward abstraction in characterdrawing," which is usually taken to be blameworthy by critics who habitually judge from a "low mimetic" standard, that is, from the standpoint of having accepted realism as the sine qua non of literature. Complaints about Morris's shortcomings in characterization are irrelevant to any intelligent attempt to understand what is going on in his work. Paul Thompson's comment, for example, that there is "never any real inner complexity" in the development of character in *The Earthly Paradise* is beside the point in an appreciation of this orchestration of mythical themes.[12]

The "realistic," unvarnished brutality that is the most salient feature of some of Morris's early poems, notably "The Haystack in the Floods," is probably the quality that has caused these poems commonly to be ranked as Morris's most significant poetic achievements.

[11] Thomas Hardy, *The Return of the Native* (London, 1968), p. 197; Frye, *Anatomy of Criticism: Four Essays* (Princeton, N.J., 1957), pp. 136–38.
[12] *Work of William Morris*, p. 175.

But although he could always write with gusto of violence,the bloodier the better, Morris never had a fully developed gift for realism, that child of the nineteenth century. According to May Morris, her father found the "elaborate realism and character study" of the "modern play" to be "intolerable." She quotes Sydney Cockerell's recollections of Morris's remarks on the drama: "Disagreeable persons should not be introduced . . . , and heroines should always be pretty." According to Cockerell, Morris "did not take to" *Tess of the D'Urbervilles*, calling it "grim," though Hardy had sent it to him after Morris's complaint in a lecture that "no one ever described real life in England." Werner Jaeger's remark about Homer, that he did not "inhabit a rationalized world, full of the banal and the commonplace," applies as well to Morris.[13] And banality can result from too much rationality, as we see in Ibsen's euhemeristic play based on the story of Sigurd, *The Vikings at Helgeland* (1858), in which, though supernatural elements are not entirely eliminated, the wonder and excitement of the traditional mythic events are totally flattened by the playwright's realistic approach.

Paradoxically, the most striking characteristic of the Pre-Raphaelite school of painting, which influenced the young Morris so profoundly, was the painstaking realism nurtured by Ruskin's tutelage.[14] But Morris was not able to train himself to paint in this fashion or to make truly realistic designs. All his designs, early and late, are stylized, even symbolic, representations of natural objects—birds, leaves, and flowers. This same stylization is what gradually takes over in his writing after the realistic *Defence of Guenevere* poems. (That social consciousness which is the second most significant aspect of Pre-Raphaelitism was the seed that fell on fertile ground. It remained with Morris until the end and, as we have seen, is evident in all his writings. But Morris would probably have developed a concern for society and a commitment to action without the Pre-Raphaelite movement. It is ironic that Rossetti, whose personal magnetism initially attracted Morris to the movement, was the least influenced, among all the Brotherhood, by either pictorial realism or social consciousness, either in his poetry or paintings. His unfinished painting, *Found*, and the poem "Jenny" are the most notable examples of his attempts in the direction of social consciousness; it is not by these that he is remembered.)

---

[13] May Morris, *Works*, XXII, xxvii–xxx; Henderson, p. 344; Jaeger, *Paideia*, I, 51.

[14] Watkinson observes that Pre-Raphaelite painting was revolutionary in that it invited comparison with life rather than fixed ideals, reflecting the nineteenth-century discovery that art and ornament were ultimately "derived from some actual observed fragment of the real world" (*Pre–Raphaelite Art and Design*, pp. 175–76).

Dante Gabriel Rossetti: *Found*. (Courtesy of the Delaware Art Museum Samuel and Mary R. Bancroft Collection.)

As for psychological realism, Morris's abiding childlike faith in man's innate goodness did not predispose him to that fascination with the mixture of good and bad qualities in humans that makes the fiction of Henry James, for instance, the tortuous triumph that it is. To Morris, so much preoccupation with the psychological and moral subtleties of conflicting motives would have been morbid. It is not surprising that he found himself unable to finish his realistic modern novel concerned with conflicting loyalties. Morris's realism is that of the Middle Ages and the early Renaissance, in which, in the words of Ian Watt, "it is universals, classes or abstractions, and not the particular, concrete objects of sense-perception, which are the true 'realities.'"[15] This is not the realism of the novel, which is based on particularities and individualities. Morris was a *pattern*-maker in several senses—he saw the universal patterns underlying individual particularities.

The striking absence in Morris of any talent, early or late, for comedy or satire, is another signal that realism was never Morris's métier. Returning to our earlier comparison, we have only to remember Hardy's rustics bumbling in and out of his tragic plots (for instance, Christopher Cantle in *The Return of the Native*) to realize how differently these authors present their "messages." Morris's most nearly realistic published literary effort, *News from Nowhere*, is good-natured in tone but completely devoid of anything that could be regarded as humor. This is not to say that Morris the man did not have his lighthearted moments, though, to judge from the available biographical material, these moments were often as not keynoted by Dickensian comments such as Joe Gargery's "Wot larks!"—giving rise to the suspicion that fragile manifestations of the comic spirit may be fatally overborne by the reading of Dickens. He preferred clipping the hedge at Kelmscott Manor into the shape of a dragon to amuse his children to the caricaturing of his friends and enemies in print.[16]

Morris's habitual use of the mythic, romantic, and high mimetic modes (again, in Northrop Frye's terms) as opposed to the low mimetic or ironic modes typically used by his Victorian contemporaries is a manifestation of his atavism. For, as most theorists agree, the movement of Western literature since premedieval times has been away from the mythical and toward the realistic, specifically the ironic. (That is, away from romance and toward the novel. But this

---

[15] *The Rise of the Novel: Studies in Defoe, Richardson, and Fielding* (Berkeley and Los Angeles, 1967), p. 11.

[16] May Morris's reminiscences about the dragon as well as an illustration of the hedge are included in *Works*, IV, xvii and facing.

tendency may be reversing itself with the current proliferation of science fiction and heroic fantasy. These, and the humble western romances, all descended from the pulp fiction of earlier decades, have more in common with the symbolic characterizations of Morris than with the superficially realistic heroes of Trollope and Dickens.)[17] Because Morris's method is anachronistic, it was not understood in his day and, I suggest, is little understood in our day when Morris's fame, like that of his heroes, is a thing of the past.

Much of the current lack of understanding is attributable to the habit of explaining the work of the Pre-Raphaelities in particular and the Victorians in general in terms of a vaguely conceived Romantic inheritance. Since there is even now no general agreement on exactly what is meant by "Romanticism," the term is of doubtful value in describing the attitudes or styles of poets who, most critics agree, were reacting in large measure against the literary postures of the second generation of Romantic poets. Such an ambitious project as attempting a definition of Romanticism, least of all detailing the philosophies of individual Romantic poets, is beyond the scope of this study. But there are some distinctions that may be made between the worlds depicted by these poets and by Morris.

The affinities between the Pre-Raphaelites and the Romantics are most obvious in the choice of subject matter, and it is true that the second generation of Romantic poets were fond of the "mythical mode" to which Morris was attracted. And, in the sense that the Victorians were, like the Romantics, attempting to create through their own efforts "a marvellous harmony of words which will integrate man, nature, and God," Morris can be seen as an inheritor of the nineteenth-century dilemma of God's disappearance, which was apprehended by the Romantics.[18] But the fundamental difference between Morris and the Romantics is in his reaction to the world of the nineteenth century. Whereas Coleridge, Wordsworth, and even Shelley withdrew from their early political activism and turned to poetry, Morris's direction was just the reverse. Romantic poetry is sometimes called the "poetry of consolation," a phrase that implies the hopelessness of real action, but Morris's poems and tales can hardly be termed consoling (except for the comforting way in which good triumphs in the romances). They are, rather, calls to action. His preoccupation with mutability and mortality, so evident in his earlier work, is, in the final analysis, turned to the end of inculcating suitable attitudes for dealing with the terrible contradictions of

[17] See Frye, pp. 33–34. See also Frye's *Secular Scripture: A Study of the Structure of Romance* (Cambridge, Mass., 1976), pp. 42–43.

[18] Miller, p. 14.

human life so that man can get on with the work at hand. In his seemingly most escapist work, *The Earthly Paradise*, he calls on his readers to set aside their yearnings for what cannot be and to deal forthrightly with both life and death, accepting the roles given them by destiny. And his own life exemplified his teachings—turning from a dead love, he immersed himself in work.

Another contrast between Morris's outlook and that of the Romantics can be seen in the difference between the Byronic hero and the Morrisian hero. There are analogies, to be sure. The Byronic hero typically embodies a symbolic guilt that makes him emblematic of fallen mankind; yet he is never reconciled to the society of man and thus can never redeem it. In *Don Juan* the paradisaical interludes in which Juan finds innocent bliss in physical love are extrasocietal and are inevitably destroyed by the intervention of a figure of autocracy (the husband or father), representing societal institutions. Further, Byron's cynical view of society is shown in the symbolic figures he chooses to represent it—Haidée's father is a pirate and Don Alfonso is a ridiculously jealous middle-aged cuckold. There is a bifurcation in the Byronic hero between the individual, which he never ceases to be, and the society to which he is related, and it is the tension between these aspects of Romantic heroism that constitutes the Byronic paradox.

But there is no such schism of identity in the Morrisian hero—here Morris's mythical method is an effective aid to meaning. Because the hero is never individualized in any realistic sense, never (to quote Burne-Jones's explanation of the expressionlessness of the subjects of his own paintings) degraded into "portraits which stand for nothing," his personal identity never becomes an obstacle to his complete reconciliation to society.[19] In other words, whereas the Romantic poets tend to present the individual as distinct or even alienated from society, suspended, as it were, in a purposeless cosmos (though there is much disagreement about the validity of this view of the Romantics), Morris's primary concern is to show the essential relationship of the individual to the plan of destiny as it is manifested in terms of human society. This is not to say that nineteenth-century hero worship in general owes nothing to the Romantics; on the contrary, as Walter E. Houghton has pointed out, the Romantic concept of the superior individual was an indispensable factor in the development of this pervasive complex of attitudes.[20] Morris would have imbibed his enthusiasm for heroes through the writings of Scott and Carlyle,

---

[19] Lord David Cecil, *Visionary and Dreamer: Two Poetic Painters: Samuel Palmer and Edward Burne-Jones* (Princeton, N.J., 1969), p. 148.

[20] *The Victorian Frame of Mind* (New Haven, 1957), pp. 305 ff.

both of whom influenced him profoundly. As Houghton notes, by the time of Victoria, the concept of the hero had become merged with the national wish for a savior; after Carlyle, the hero is conceived to be inextricably bound to society.

If it is true, as Robert Langbaum states, that the "romanticist sees the past as different from the present and uses the past to explore the full extent of the difference, the full extent in other words of his own modernity," then it is clear that Morris departs from the Romantics in his use of the past as a literary subject.[21] For Morris does not use the past "to give meaning to an admittedly meaningless world." The cumulative message of Morris's reiterated emphasis on fate is that there is a meaning in human affairs and that it is the work of man to allow this meaning to be made manifest in his own life through the subordination of his individual will to destiny. The past is, in the Morrisian world, a paradigm of the present and the future, for history does repeat itself and can never be divorced from what is now. There is a superficial similarity and a basic difference between Morris's fascination with dead and dying civilizations and the more typically Romantic interest of Rossetti. "The Burden of Nineveh," one of Rossetti's most striking poems, expresses what Oswald Doughty calls "the apparently endless deceptions of humanity by Fate, the futility of human beliefs, the apparent meaninglessness of the Universe from a human standpoint."[22]

Langbaum's distinction between the romantic and the classical sense of the past—"the romanticist does not see the present as the heir of the past and does not therefore look to the past for authority as an ethical model"—would identify Morris as a classicist rather than a romanticist.[23] Insofar as any categories are useful for understanding, this one is just as appropriate, in some respects, as romanticism. For Morris's constant reiteration of the golden age theme, implying as it does the deterioration of man's state since that paradisaical time and the need for emulation of the values of the past, is very close to the golden age theme as used by Pope, especially in his *Pastorals*, and

---

[21] *The Poetry of Experience: The Dramatic Monologue in Modern Literary Tradition* (New York, 1957), p. 12.

[22] "Dante Gabriel Rossetti," in *British Writers and Their Work*, No. 7, ed. Bonamy Dobrée and T. O. Beachcroft (Lincoln, Neb.: Univ. of Nebraska Press, 1965), p. 20.

[23] Langbaum, p. 12. My suggestion that Morris might be regarded as a classicist actually parallels, on a literary level, Peter Floud's more serious revisionist argument that "Morris must be regarded as the great classical designer of his age . . . while others searched for more novel and unorthodox solutions to the problems of design" ("William Morris as an Artist: A New View," p. 564). It would be unfair not to call attention to Morris's well-documented contempt for the art and literature of the eighteenth century, for which see May Morris, *William Morris: Artist, Writer, Socialist*, II, 630–31, and Lemire, pp. 68–70 ("The Gothic Revival [I]").

recalls the ancients versus moderns controversy of the seventeenth and eighteenth centuries. Dryden freely used analogies between the present and the past as basic metaphors for his poetry, as in "Astraea Redux," wherein the accession of Charles II is seen as a renewal of the reign of Saturn when the Virgin, Justice, returns, and even in the satirical "Absalom and Achitophel," which is based upon a comparison approaching actual identification of Charles with David.

One could go on pointing out similarities in theme and outlook between Morris and poets of other ages and climes (Spenser was mentioned briefly earlier) simply because Morris worked in a tradition of great antiquity and popularity. The point is that Morris's poetry is in the main tradition of Western literature, which has typically been written in the belief that literature has something to do with life. For the divorce of art and life, which the aesthetes attempted to effect, is a modern phenomenon, one that is not germane to the study of Morris, who spent a large part of his life trying to reintroduce into Victorian society what to him was a natural and essential relationship. Morris's advice in "The Beauty of Life" (XXII, 77), "Have nothing in your houses which you do not know to be useful or believe to be beautiful," may be contrasted with Gautier's pronouncement in his Preface to *Mademoiselle de Maupin* (1835): "There is nothing truly beautiful but that which can never be of any use whatsoever; everything useful is ugly, for it is the expression of some need, and man's needs are ignoble and disgusting like his own poor and infirm nature. The most useful place in a house is the water-closet."[24] Morris's lecture "Art and the Beauty of the Earth," delivered in 1881, is a call to revolution, that is, a reinstatement of the ancient integration of art and life:

But first, lest any of you doubt it, let me ask you what forms the great mass of the objects that fill our museums, setting aside positive pictures and sculpture? Is it not just the common household goods of past time? True it is that some people may look upon them simply as curiosities, but you and I have been taught most properly to look upon them as priceless treasures that can teach us all sorts of things, and yet, I repeat, they are for the most part common household goods, wrought by "common fellows," as people say now, without any cultivation, men who thought the sun went round the earth, and that Jerusalem was exactly in the middle of the world. [XXII, 162]

Morris's poetry and prose writings are consonant with his views on art and society. They are no more escapist than the *Iliad* and the *Odyssey*. Like the Homeric epics, they are neither topical nor overtly didactic, but educative in the sense of inculcating ideals of heroic

[24] Théophile Gautier, *Mademoiselle de Maupin* (New York, 1944), p. xxx.

attitudes and behavior. As he said of himself, he was no "mere praiser of past times" (XXII, 163); his mission was to redeem the world. Like all the Victorians, Morris failed in his attempt to show the world a better way. Because their society could not learn from them, we, the inheritors of the world, struggle with the same problems the sages sought to solve. But Morris's failure does not invalidate his philosophy—he accepted his role as he saw it and threw himself heroically into the fray. The outcome belongs to destiny.

Index

Index